Retire Rich and Happy

12 "Secrets" to
Retirement Success

Jeffrey B. Harris

Aames-Abbott Publishing

Disclaimer...

This publication is designed to provide accurate, authoritative information on the subject matter covered. It is not intended as legal, accounting or investment advice and readers should seek the counsel of appropriate professionals before acting on any of the recommendations herein. At the time of this writing the author is an independent contractor with Raymond James Financial Services, Inc. of St. Petersburg, Florida, member NASD/SIPC. However, neither Ramyond James, Inc. nor any of its subsidiaries endorse this book or will be held liable for any claims made against it.

Jeff Harris & Associates, Inc.
410 Neff Ave. Suite 200
Harrisonburg, VA 22801
Phone   540-574-2508
Fax   540-433-3561
www.retirerich-online.com

Published by: **Aames-Abbott Publishing**
131 Mariners Bluff Rd.
York, SC 29745
(803) 980-1993

Printed in the United States of America

ISBN: 0-9769565-090000

To DeAnn,

My wife, best friend and biggest cheerleader!

All my love.

Foreword

Jeff Harris was introduced to me by a mutual friend, Ty Boyd, the renowned speaker and communications coach from Charlotte, North Carolina. As soon as I met Jeff, I recognized the seeds of greatness in him and was thrilled when he asked me to write the foreword for his first book.

When I heard Jeff Harris' story and read this book, I saw similarities to my own life's journey. Like Jeff, I started poor, with the odds stacked against me. Like Jeff, I worked hard, saved, and using many of the "secrets" explained in this book, was able to make my dream of a better life come true.

Today, as Chairman of Great Harvest Bread Company and President of High Point University and as an active volunteer in many non-profits, I understand the value and substance of what Jeff teaches.

This book shows that anyone can achieve extraordinary results by learning and applying sound principles.

Don't be fooled by the simplicity of some of the "secrets" Jeff reveals. They may seem simple at first, but when applied, they are very powerful and could dramatically change your life for the better.

What I liked about this book is that it's down to earth, practical, and based on real life, not theory. Jeff doesn't try to impress you with fancy words or industry jargon. He clearly and succinctly articulates what works and just as important, what doesn't.

In reading it, I could tell that Jeff was drawing upon a deep reservoir of professional expertise and knowledge gained from many years of practical hands-on experience.

I believe it's vitally important for people to understand sound financial management concepts. Such knowledge enables you to embrace opportunities that come your way, and avoid the pitfalls along life's highway.

Read it, apply it, and enjoy the results!

Nido Qubein
High Point, North Carolina

www.Nidoqubein.com

Acknowledgements

No one ever prospers without the willing help of others, and this book is no exception. My life has been filled with amazing blessings and I want to thank my God, family and friends for their help, love and encouragement.

In particular I want to thank my editor, Mike Hernacki, who patiently guided me. To all my draft reviewers: Howard Anderson, CPA; Sandy Cereola, CPA; Tom McThenia, JD; Jeff Lenhart, JD; Steve Heitz, JD; Brooks Marshall, PhD; Dick Roberds, PhD; Dane Cox, PhD; Kevin O'Connor; Nido Qubein; Cyndi Maxey; David Bilyeu; Jeff Thull; Roz Usheroff; Merle Shank; Ann Elliott; Dan Poynter; Rich Lynch; Roxanne Emmerich and Tom Antion.

I want to thank my personal assistant, Jean Brunk, for all her help so I could have the time to devote to writing. Thanks to all my clients who encouraged me during the process, and who gave me the opportunity to be of service.

I want to thank my wife, DeAnn, for gently prodding me to finally write this book and quit talking about it.

Thanks to my daughters, Melissa, Meloney and Miriam, for growing up to be beautiful, godly women I'm proud of.

I want to thank my Dad, Walton Harris, for teaching me the power of honesty, the joy of laughter and how to cook delicious "suck-off-the-bone" hickory-smoked barbeque ribs.

Finally a big thank you to Steve Acker and Wayne Beddow of Charlottesville, Virginia. Without your help none of this would have been possible.

Jeff Harris

Where Are All the Endorsements for This Book?

This is usually the "Praise Page" where you'd find all kinds of ringing endorsements for the book. Things like: "An incredible masterpiece of literary genius!" or "Amazing! Every personal library should have a copy of *Retire Rich And Happy*. You can't live without it!"

Well, not in this case. I'm not a financial journalist with First Amendment freedoms to say virtually anything I want. The investment advisory industry is highly regulated by the states and by the Securities and Exchange Commission (SEC). That's why you'll see the statement, "Past performance is no guarantee of future results," repeated ad nauseam every time I cite historical data in this book.

Practicing professionals like myself are held to very high standards as fiduciaries. We are obligated by law to put our clients' interests ahead of our own. Therefore we must be very careful to abide by SEC rules.

One of those rules is: **Rule 206(4)-1** under the Advisers Act—**The Advertising Rule**. In short, this rule prohibits Investment Advisor Representatives from using endorsements.

So you won't see any of the usual *Amazing! Incredible! Stupendous!* endorsements that commonly fill up this page. I'll leave it up to you, the reader, to determine for yourself the value of this book.

My hope is that after you're done, you'll think, "That *was* an amazing, incredible book. It has changed my life! Every personal library *should* have a copy of *Retire Rich and Happy*." Then you'll go out and tell your friends about it. That's the best endorsement any author could hope for.

Jeff Harris

Who Should Read This Book?

You should read this book if:

- You own a successful business, or are married to someone who does.*

- You want to live a full, meaningful life of significance.

- You want to accumulate substantial financial resources so you can be free to do what you want, when you want.

- Your time is limited, and you place a high value on your free hours.

- You want to Retire Rich <u>and</u> Happy.

I know you're busy, so this book isn't very long. And it's filled with graphs and real-life stories that make for easy reading. I've tried to keep the Wall Street lingo to a minimum. When I have to use a financial term you might not know, I explain what it means right away.

Don't Waste Your Time

If you're already an investment whiz, or you think you are, don't bother reading this book. Give it to a business-owner friend who recognizes their limitations and understands the principle of delegation.

This book is based on a fundamental premise: As a business owner, you should focus on running your business, because that's what you're good at. That means you should delegate everything else to competent, trustworthy associates, and pay them well.

If you're a "bottom line" type of person, just read the summary at the beginning of each chapter. If you read all the summaries, it shouldn't take you more than 10 minutes total—and could quite literally change your life! You can read the rest when you take your next vacation.

---

* When I first began writing this book I focused it exclusively on business owners. But my CPA and attorney friends, after reviewing initial drafts of the book, suggested the concepts and ideas were generally just as applicable to non-business owners also.

In this book, you'll discover:

- The power of beginning with your ideal retirement lifestyle in mind;

- How to avoid being a workaholic and live the life you've always dreamed of;

- Why you should delegate the investment process to trained professionals;

- How to identify a knowledgeable, trustworthy "investment advocate;"

- Why normal human emotions sabotage most do-it-yourself investors;

- Why you should have a "Money Map;"

- What fee range is reasonable for investment advice;

- How to turn your retirement plan into a cash-flow machine to give you financial freedom;

- How to protect yourself from unlimited personal liability when your company sponsors a qualified retirement plan;

- How you can bless your family and change the world for the better with your retirement plan funds;

- How to live a fulfilling, enjoyable, balanced life now and when you retire.

The Secrets I refer to in the book aren't really "secrets" in that very few people know about them. Everything in this book is fairly common knowledge *in the investment industry*. If you've been around money for a while, you've probably at least heard about some of these "secrets."

But in almost a quarter-century in the financial services business, I've found that much of what people like me deal with every day is completely foreign to people like you. The language is foreign, too—like when I listen to two physicians talk and haven't a clue what they're saying. ("His rectosteophats are 200 and climbing! Should we disconsulivate his PTS?") So for you, the concepts in this book may well be "secrets"—but they're secrets you *should* know.

Cutting Through the Mystery

This book is designed to cut through the mystery that surrounds prudent retirement plan investing. It reveals "secrets" and strategies that have worked for many other business owners—people like you, who know how to make a business successful and want to enjoy the fruits of that success for the rest of their days by retiring not only rich, but Rich <u>and</u> Happy.

I'm honored that you're taking the time to read this book. I hope it will empower you to take charge of your retirement plan assets and ensure they are being well-managed for your benefit. In my years of investment management consulting, I've witnessed the many mistakes and outright disasters that befall so many well-meaning, but ill-informed business owners when it comes to managing their retirement plan money.

That doesn't have to happen to you. You've worked too long and hard to let your money slip through your fingers. Now you have a resource that can help you ask the right questions and take the necessary steps to develop a successful investment process. If this book does what I hope, it will help you create a happy, healthy, abundant life and retirement for you and your family.

Jeffrey B. Harris, ChFC
Registered Principal
Raymond James Financial Services, Inc.
Registered Investment Advisor
Jeff Harris & Associates, Inc.

www.raymondjames.com/jharris

About the Author

Jeff Harris grew up near Richmond, Virginia and attended Bridgewater College. He married his high school sweetheart, DeAnn, and needing income, worked in a junkyard while they began their family, which eventually grew to three daughters. Later, he stocked shelves in a supermarket and his career seemed to be headed nowhere.

But then he went to an office Christmas party that changed his life forever. He met a young stockbroker who started telling Jeff about mutual funds. At the time, his entire financial strategy involved putting part of his paycheck into a savings account. When the broker explained that some mutual funds had been averaging twice the returns he got from the bank, Jeff was hooked.

He started to read everything he could about investing, and soon began moving his money from the bank to mutual funds recommended by the broker. He was so enthusiastic about his new-found strategy that he began telling all his friends and co-workers about it. He referred so many new clients to the broker that his firm offered Jeff a part-time job.

He jumped at the chance and began his financial services career in 1981. Two years later, he began working full-time for a small brokerage firm. Operating out of his home, with no salary, Jeff found the first five years extremely difficult. But he stuck with it, earned the title of Regional Vice President and opened a branch office in Charlottesville, Virginia. The following year he founded Jeff Harris & Associates, Inc. to offer independent financial advice.

In 1989, Jeff moved his family and business to Harrisonburg, Virginia and started teaching retirement planning workshops as an adjunct professor at Blue Ridge Community College and later at James Madison University. Always active in professional organizations, Jeff was president of the Virginia Society of Certified Public Accountants Blue Ridge Chapter, 2002-03. In 2004 Jeff and DeAnn moved to Lake Wylie, South Carolina, near Charlotte, North Carolina. Jeff maintains offices in Harrisonburg, Virginia and Charlotte.

Unlike many financial writers who only report on personal finance, Jeff actually works in the industry every day. In 1999 he partnered with

Raymond James Financial Services, Inc. (RJFS) of St. Petersburg, Florida. This relationship enables Jeff to bring the resources and strength of its affiliate, Raymond James & Associates, Inc., a New York Stock Exchange member firm, and its nationally-recognized parent company, Raymond James Financial, Inc., to work for his clients.

Jeff is a Registered Principal with Raymond James Financial Services, Inc. (Member NASD/SIPC), manages his branch office in Harrisonburg, VA and serves his clients nationwide.

Jeff particularly enjoys working with business owners who've built their business over time. He says, "Since I started out working in a junkyard and grocery store, I understand the value of a dollar and the importance of hard work. Nobody handed me anything when I started and I had no connections. I like working with business owners because they appreciate and value what I can do for them."

Jeff enjoys flying, cooking, military history and fitness. He has over 1,100 hours as an instrument-rated private pilot and often volunteers his time to fly Angel Flights (see related article in Appendix A).

Jeff and DeAnn believe strongly in charitable giving and have created the Harris Family Donor-Advised Fund to support a variety of charitable organizations. Both are involved in church activities. Jeff has served as an Elder at Grace Covenant Church in Harrisonburg, VA. He and DeAnn attend Morningstar Fellowship Church near Charlotte, NC and are both certified Chaplains, serving the business community.

Professional Development

Chartered Financial Consultant (ChFC), American College in Bryn Mawr, PA, 1996

Completed the Abbts Institute of Estate Planning Course, 1997

Completed the Raymond James Trust School, 2000

Certified Wealth Manager (CWM) designation, Canon School of Wealth Management, Northwestern University, 2002

Accredited Investment Fiduciary (AIF) designation, Center for Fiduciary Studies, University of Pittsburgh, 2003

Retire Rich and Happy

12 Secrets to Retirement Success
Table of Contents

SECRET #1

What a Day for a Daydream

To create your ideal retirement, begin with the end in mind

What you'll discover in this chapter:

☞ If you want to achieve a rich and happy retirement, it's critically important to begin with your ideal retirement lifestyle in mind.

☞ Make up your mind to enjoy every day right now! You have no guarantees for tomorrow.

☞ If you could wave a magic wand, what would your ideal life and retirement look like?

☞ Don't lose sight of the most important things in life: family, friends, health, spiritual and personal growth.

☞ You will become what you think about and focus on—good or bad.

If you want to retire rich, and you own a business, your retirement plan is an important tool. It can provide an income stream to support you in style the rest of your life. But if you want to retire Rich <u>and</u> Happy, you need to do much more than just put money into a retirement plan.

As I've worked with successful business owners like you over the years, I've noticed something interesting. Often they'll get so caught up in the busy-ness of day-to-day living that they completely miss out on the most important things in life. Most business owners succeed well enough to fund a comfortable retirement, yet fail to give serious thought to what they want their retirement lifestyle to look like.

If you want to retire Rich and Happy, that is…

■ to accumulate the assets necessary to live a full, meaningful, productive life during your retirement years;

■ to leave behind something of real value;

■ to live a life of triumph, not tragedy…

…you must have a solid *plan* for achieving the life you want.

And every good plan begins with a dream, a vision, a mental picture of what you want your life to look like. If you know what you want your ideal retirement years to look like, *and focus on that image,* it will be much easier to accumulate the financial resources to fulfill your dream.

This might sound like self-help psychobabble, but it's not. The idea of *beginning with the end in mind* isn't new. It's based on the experience and observations of numerous scholars and thinkers dating back thousands of years:

For as he thinks in his heart, so is he…
  Proverbs 23:7 (Amplified Bible)

We are shaped by our thoughts; we become what we think.
  Buddha, *The Dharmapada*
  Indian philosopher & religious leader (563 BC - 483 BC)

The universe is change; our life is what our thoughts make it.
  Marcus Aurelius Antoninus, *Meditations*
  Roman Emperor, A.D. 161-180 (121 AD - 180 AD)

We become what we think about all day long.
  Ralph Waldo Emerson
  US essayist & poet (1803 - 1882)

You are today where your thoughts have brought you;
you will be tomorrow where your thoughts take you.
  James Lane Allen
  American novelist, 1849-1925

Every major religion acknowledges this truth. Every inspirational speaker and writer says it sooner or later. The legendary Earl Nightingale recorded the only non-musical album ever to go "gold." He called it "The Strangest Secret," and his message was: *You become what you think about. You create what you focus on.*

If you get nothing else out of this book, I hope this "secret" sticks with you, because in many ways it's the most important.

I know because it happened to me. Let me tell you the story.

Don't Wait to Live Your Ideal Life; Learn How to Do It *Now*!

Early in my career I was extremely focused on financial success and was willing to pay any price to reach my goals. (Does that sound at all like you?) Anyway, the hard work paid off, and after a while I began to experience the financial rewards and recognition that came with career success.

But I sensed something important was lacking. My business was doing well; I had a nice family and a bright future. Yet I was not really enjoying my life. I was becoming richer, but not happier. Because I was so focused on business, I failed to notice that my relationship with my wife was suffering. Also, I hadn't spent much time with our three daughters, so I didn't really know them very well.

Then two defining events occurred that caused me to re-evaluate my priorities.

The first came on Easter Sunday, 1991. After church I decided to call my older brother Steve to wish him a Happy Easter. I hoped to cheer him up because his job wasn't going well, his wife had asked him to move out, and things were tense at home. His seven-year-old daughter answered the phone and said her Daddy was still sleeping, so I said I'd call back later.

That afternoon, my wife DeAnn and I went hiking in the Blue Ridge Mountains and I forgot to call Steve back. Just after we'd gone to bed that night our phone rang. My mother was sobbing so hard, I could barely make out her words: "Your brother Steve is dead!"

Time seemed to stand still and I felt like I was in a mind-numbed fog. My brother dead? That can't be; he's only 39, and he was fine this morning!

The autopsy revealed my brother had heart disease, the silent killer. He'd been mowing his lawn that afternoon when his heart skipped a beat, then just stopped.

It wasn't fair! He should have had many more years to get his life straightened out. Fair or not, the hard reality was my only brother was dead, and there would be no more "second chances" to live the life he'd always wanted.

I wish I could say this tragic experience caused me to immediately change my focus, but it didn't. Too quickly, I fell back into the familiar embrace of my frenetic work routine.

In those days, I was teaching at a local university and hosting a weekly live call-in radio show on personal finance. Every weekend I wrote, edited and taped a personal finance segment for our local TV station. I edited and produced a monthly newsletter. And of course, I worked with my clients. What was *really* happening was, I was killing myself and ignoring my most important relationships.

The Clock Starts Ticking For My "Wake-Up" Call

It wasn't until six years later that the second defining event occurred, changing me for good. I'd taken my wife, daughters and parents to Hawaii on a trip I had won for my hard work. Shortly after our return, my Dad hurt his back.

He was upset because the doctor told him he couldn't drive his brand new Cadillac Eldorado. This was his dream car and he loved it. All his life he'd talked of buying a brand new Cadillac and finally, at age 73, he'd done it.

Sadly, he never drove that car again. Instead of getting better, be grew worse. He went to another doctor, who discovered that Dad had cancer. Just eight weeks later, he was dead.

We had been very close, and his death hit me hard. I began thinking deeply about the really important things in life, and how I was missing out on so much because I was caught up with business concerns. My plan had been to work hard, build my business up, and then retire financially independent so I could live however I chose.

It began to dawn on me that I had no guarantees for the future. My brother Steve was gone. His future died at age 39. My Dad was gone, and even though he'd lived into his 70's, he missed out on a lot of things he had hoped to experience, like that car. I realized that if I didn't start living, really living, a full, joyful life right now, I might never have the opportunity to do so!

A Radical Decision

So I hired a business consultant to help me manage my business more effectively. The first thing he had me do was create a list of my most difficult clients. Then he told me to politely disengage from the relationships that weren't working. He explained that there were some people whom I would never be able to please regardless of how hard I tried, that they would be better off working with someone else—and I would have much more peace. (Notice the important word here is "peace," not "income.")

Next, he had me reduce my schedule so I was seeing clients only two days a week. Finally, he had me focus my efforts so I was working only with those clients who could benefit most from my services. The other days I could focus on all the issues that required my close attention without being distracted with client meetings.

At first, this sounded radical, dangerous and impossible. But as I began to implement the changes, I saw my business becoming even more successful.

That's right; with fewer clients and a shorter work week, I was actually making more money. If you're a workaholic, or just overworked right now, read the previous sentence again. There's a message in it for you.

A New Life Opens Up

I was loving my new-found freedom and really starting to enjoy life! I took up flying as a hobby, and because I had more time, I earned my license in just four months.

DeAnn and I attended a marriage seminar, strengthening and deepening our relationship as never before. With my new free time I was able to become more active in church, and accepted an offer to serve as an Elder.

Over the years I've discovered that like the "old me," many people are waiting to begin living the life they've always dreamed of *some time in the distant future.* "I'll really start enjoying life when: (check the blank) ____ the kids leave; ____ I've sold the business; ____ we've saved enough money; ____ we go public." Insert your own excuse here:

_____

As I learned from bitter experience, *nobody* has any guarantee about the future, so you'd better start living the life you've always dreamed about *right now.*

Granted, you might not be able to retire today. But you can choose what's most important to you. The choices you make today will shape your future just as surely as blueprints dictate the shape of a new building. So it's important—no, it's vitally important—to give careful thought now to what you want your future retirement years to look like, and start giving shape to that image.

Retiring WITHOUT the End in Mind

Because it's so important, I'll say it again: *Begin with the end in mind.* The vast majority of business owners never learn this simple but amazing secret. Their lives are filled with hectic days of putting out fires, running full-speed, reacting to the crisis of the moment.

They're working hard and often making piles of money. But their stress level is high, their satisfaction level is low. They're getting rich, but deep down they're not very happy.

Often they think that if they could just retire and put all this pressure behind them, life would be great! So they sell the business or hire a manager to run it and start taking an income from their retirement plan. They're ready to enjoy the good life!

A few weeks or months into their "retirement," a sad realization sets in. After years of neglecting their marriage, children, health, spiritual life, friends and community, they feel lonely, hollow and empty.

They have time, but all they ever used their time for was work, and now that they don't have work, they have nothing. Retirement isn't turning out to be the "good life" they thought it would be.

Some will put the blame on others: "My wife doesn't have time for me and is always off with her friends. My children are bitter and rebellious, so I really can't get to know them. I never had time to develop any genuinely close friendships, so I don't have anyone to hang out with."

Others will try to use their long-accumulating pile of money to buy happiness. But money can't buy a close, loving, fulfilling marriage. It can't make your children want to spend time with you. It can't buy you good health, or true friends, or a strong relationship with your Creator.

Ironically, money turns out to be one of the least important components of a fulfilling, meaningful, retirement. Specialists in the growing field of retirement planning report that people who are nearing retirement list money as their #1 concern. When interviewed some time after they retire, those same people say that money turned out to be among the least of their troubles. Yes, money is important, but not at the expense of the *really* important things in life.

How to Use This Secret

It all starts with a dream. I titled this chapter, "What a Day for a Daydream" because a daydream is the first step in creating a successful retirement plan. And the day to do that is TODAY.

You don't have to sit down and plan exactly what you'll do every minute of your retirement. Just start out using your non-logical, imaginative "right brain," daydreaming or imagining what life might look like if you were retired. See yourself spending your time doing what you most enjoy. Start writing down some ideas.

Talk to your spouse and other important people in your life. Find out what their dream lifestyle would look like and see how your visions coincide or differ. From time to time, stop and picture what you'd be doing during a perfect day of retirement. Let your imagination go. Don't limit yourself. Let yourself experience the *ideal*.

Maybe you're not good at dreaming. Could be your imagination needs a jump start. I've found that asking myself a series of questions helps kick my brain into gear so I can visualize an ideal life and retirement.

Here's a general question: If you could wave a magic wand and *live the life you've always dreamed of* now and during your retirement years, what would that ideal life look like? The answers to that question will form the basis for a more complete retirement picture.

Once you've got your imagination going, you can get more specific, with questions like:

- Where would I live? On the beach, lake or mountains?
- Whom would I be living with (or without)?
- What would my home look like?
- Would I have more than one home?
- How would I be spending most of my time?
- In order to do these things, how healthy, vital and energetic would I need to be?
- What would I do to stay healthy, mentally and physically?
- What would my spiritual life look like?
- What would I do to grow spiritually?
- How strong would my relationship be with my spouse, children and grandchildren?
- How could I help my children and grandchildren learn universal laws and truths that will guide them to live a full, meaningful abundant life?
- How can I keep my children and grandchildren from becoming spoiled?
- What would my family and friends cherish most about me?
- How would my life change the world for the better many years in the future?

Write your answers down. Read them over. Think about them. Give this exercise some time and energy and it will focus your thinking and serve as a magnet to draw you relentlessly toward your ideal life, both now and during your retirement years.

If you're resisting taking this first step, think about this. If you're in decent health, with the help of modern medicine, you'll probably be retired for a very long time: 20, 30 years, maybe more. Isn't that long and important period in your life worth all the time and attention you can give it? Don't forget: *you create what you think about.*

Today would be the perfect time to get started. What a day for a daydream!

Remember . . .

☞ Beginning with your ideal retirement lifestyle in mind is critically important to achieving a fulfilling, joyful retirement.

☞ Determine to enjoy every day right now! Don't live for some vague future when you think everything will be wonderful.

☞ If you could wave a magic wand, what would your ideal life and retirement look like?

☞ Don't lose sight of the most important things in life, like your relationships with family and friends, your physical and spiritual health, your personal growth.

☞ You will become what you think about and focus on—good or bad.

Resource:

Go to my website, **retirerich-online.com** and click on the **"Happy"** link for more information on how to create the life and retirement you've always dreamed of.

SECRET #2

Penny-Wise, Pound-Foolish

Retirement Plan Investing is NOT a Do-It-Yourself Project

What you'll discover in this chapter:

☞ Your business is successful because you understand the power of delegation.

☞ Don't try to play portfolio manager with your retirement money. Delegate the task to a trustworthy, knowledgeable investment advocate.

☞ A quality advisor is an asset to your business, not an expense.

☞ A simple test to see if you should be managing your own retirement plan.

☞ It's bad business to be penny-wise and pound-foolish. You get what you pay for.

If you're a successful business owner, you have many important skills. One of the most important is this: *You know how to delegate.* You don't try to do everything yourself. Instead, you use the knowledge, skills, talents, strengths and resources of others to build, supply, operate and manage your business.

You realize that your time, energy and expertise are limited. So you hire others to do what *they* do well while you spend your time doing what *you* do well. That's just good business.

When it comes to investing and managing your retirement plan assets, the same idea applies. Think of your retirement plan as a separate business. In order to succeed, it demands planning, good management and attention to detail—just like your regular business.

Trouble is, running your business takes so much of your time and energy, it's hard to give much attention to how well your retirement investments are doing. So you sort of ignore them. I understand, but I have to tell you; that's a big mistake. And it's a mistake that can hide from you for years.

Here's how that happens. The regular contributions you're making to your plan usually keep the overall size of your assets growing year after year. As the plan grows, it looks like it's doing all right, but the growth in asset sizes may be masking poor performance compared to other investment choices.

You can lose two or three percent every year and not feel like it's hurting you much. But later in the book we'll see how poor long-term investment performance could cost you a small fortune—maybe even a large one!

"Our Retirement Plan's Doing OK"

Recently I ran into a textbook example of how poor investment performance can be masked by ongoing contributions. I've managed the investments for a homeowner's association for a number of years.

Pleased with our results, the board asked me to review the association's pension plan investments for their employees. However, some of the corporation's officers didn't feel this was necessary because they said, "Our retirement plan's doing OK."

The money they were adding to the plan regularly masked some big problems, but they ultimately agreed to proceed. In part, the analysis revealed the following:

- Their plan was averaging less than half the return of a properly diversified portfolio. (Secret #6)

- Their previous advisor was charging front-load commissions instead of a fee-for-service. (Secret #3)

- Their plan contained junk bond holdings (very risky) which could be considered inappropriate. (Secret #10)

- They had no Investment Policy Statement. (Secrets #5 and #10)

- Their plan was grossly over-concentrated in growth and income stock funds. (Secret #6)

Ignorance is Not Bliss

When it comes to your retirement plan investments, ignorance is not bliss—and it can ultimately be very expensive! Fortunately, we were able to bring this plan into compliance with government guidelines quite easily, thus serving to protect the officers and board members from unlimited personal liability.

Plus, we properly diversified the portfolio, which has dramatically improved the investment results. I suspect most business owners could benefit from this type of retirement plan analysis.

If everything is OK, an analysis would confirm it. If not, the problems could be identified and addressed before they got bigger. **You don't want to be penny-wise and pound-foolish with government-regulated retirement plans when you could face unlimited personal liability!**

If you're anything like the average business owner, the assets in your retirement plan are the second most valuable financial resource you own, exceeded only by the value of your business itself. Again, if you think like most owners, you figure that one day you'll sell the business and the big pile of money you'll get will fund a comfortable retirement.

That's faulty thinking. Market forces can drive the value of your business down. You could become ill and may have to sell in a hurry. When you're ready to sell, or when you have to, you might not be able to sell it profitably, if at all. Then what? Then you'll look to the assets in that retirement plan you've been ignoring all these years.

The Mistakes Business Owners Make

OK, so ignoring your plan assets is a big mistake. Another mistake is trying to manage the money yourself. Usually that involves pouring it into a mutual fund and assuming that the mutual fund company will tell you if anything needs to be changed.

Some business owners actually try to play portfolio manager and do their own research, as well as buying and selling assets as the markets change. This goes directly against what you already know to be good business practice: *delegating* important tasks to professionals.

Why don't more business owners like you delegate this job to a competent, trustworthy financial advisor? In nearly 25 years in the investment field, I've discovered five basic reasons why many business owners fail to take this crucial step;

1. You know there are competent, knowledgeable, trustworthy advisors who will put your best interests first, and you know there are commissioned salespeople who are just trying to make a fast buck. But **you don't know how to tell the difference.** So you do nothing. (see Secret #3)

2. **You expect the company who sold you your retirement plan—** a mutual fund, insurance company or brokerage firm—**to help you manage and monitor your investment choices.** Unfortunately, as you'll learn in Secret #10, these providers don't want to be considered fiduciaries, which saddles them with a much higher level of responsibility. So they generally avoid giving on-going investment advice, even though that's supposedly what they're being paid to do!

3. **You may think hiring a financial advisor would cost too much and wouldn't be worth the expense.** A high-quality advisor should be able to help you improve your investment returns net of any fee charged. In short, they should help you make money, lower your exposure to market volatility, give you valuable peace-of-mind and free your time to spend as you please. A good advisor is a business asset, (like your CPA and attorney) not an expense.

4. So many do-it-yourself investors were losing piles of retirement money in the market meltdown following March 2000, that Congress passed a new law in December 2001 allowing companies that sponsor retirement plans to hire independent financial advisors to help participants invest and manage their retirement money. **Most business owners are not aware of this new law. Were you?**

5. **You're so busy running your day-to-day business that you can't imagine adding something else to your already-overloaded schedule.** So you do nothing, and often suffer needless financial harm. However, forward-thinking, discerning business owners realize they should delegate the management of their retirement plan assets so they can focus on what they do best: running their business. (Since you're reading this book, that makes you one such owner.)

A Simple Test to See If You Should Be Managing Your Own Retirement Plan

Occasionally I'll see TV ads for Internet brokerage firms suggesting that if you have a computer with an Internet connection, you can manage your own investments just fine, as long as you subscribe to their website. That's not necessarily false advertising. The fact is, some people can and do manage their own investments very well without professional help.

But the facts also suggest that the vast majority of do-it-yourself investors don't do very well, as you'll see in Secret #4. So delegating investment decisions makes sense for most people; especially a time-crunched, successful business owner like you.

If you fancy yourself a good investment manager (and you may be), ask yourself this question: "If a business owner were reviewing the **training, qualifications** and **track record** of candidates to manage their investments, would they hire me?" If you can't think of anyone who would hand over their portfolio to you, and pay you real money for your help, then let me suggest you should not do that either. Instead, consider delegating the chore to a competent professional. Secret #3 will show you how to do so.

My father was not a financial expert, but he often told me not to be penny-wise and pound-foolish. "You get what you pay for," he said again and again.

Experience has taught me he was right. When it comes to successful retirement plan investing, the stakes are too high to risk being penny-wise. Your future and the well-being of your family are too important to leave in the hands of an amateur—even if that amateur is *you.*

Remember . . .

☞ You own a successful business because you understand the power of delegation.

☞ Don't try to play portfolio manager with your retirement money. Delegate the task to a trustworthy, knowledgeable investment advocate.

☞ A quality advisor is an asset to your business, not an expense.

☞ Based on your training, qualifications and track record, would anyone pay you to manage their retirement money?

☞ Don't be penny-wise and pound-foolish. You get what you pay for.

Resource:

To learn more about what's required of business owners who sponsor retirement plans, go to the Department of Labor's website at **http://www.dol.gov/ebsa/compliance_assistance.html**. Being penny-wise and pound-foolish now could wind up being very expensive later.

SECRET #3

The Wisdom of Solomon
Choosing Your Investment Advocate

In this chapter you'll discover why:

☞ You want your advocate's interests aligned with yours.

☞ Experience and training are vitally important.

☞ Your personality should "click" with your advocate.

☞ Your advocate doesn't have to live in your town.

☞ Your advocate should take a "whole-brain" approach to financial management.

There's an old joke about the recipe for rabbit stew. It goes like this: *First, catch a rabbit.*

In other words, the first step may be the hardest. But once you've completed that successfully, the rest can be relatively easy.

So it is with finding an investment advisor who is:

■ trustworthy,

■ knowledgeable, and

■ has a proven track record of helping clients earn reasonable returns on their retirement plans.

It may take you a while to find such a person, but when you do, you'll have a genuine advocate worth their weight in gold!

An Advocate, Not Just an Advisor

I use the word "advocate" to describe this type of advisor because you want someone who will not just give advice. You want someone who is truly on your side of the desk. Someone who has your best interests at heart, who treats your money as if it were their own.

The question is, how do you distinguish between the pretenders and the real pros? Entrusting the wrong person with your retirement money could result in financial disaster, so you must choose carefully. Unfortunately, there's no easy way to know. But by following some common-sense guidelines, you'll greatly improve your chances of finding the right advocate for you.

To the average consumer, anyone who calls themselves a "financial consultant" looks pretty much the same. Stockbrokers, insurance agents, mutual fund salesmen, investment advisor representatives, bank trust officers, credit union reps—they all can have the words "Financial Consultant" printed on their business cards.

They all have licenses permitting them to offer you some kind of financial product or service. Stockbrokers may dress a little better; insurance agents may be a little pushier; bank trust officers may act more conservative. But to the untrained observer, it's hard to tell who knows what they're doing and who doesn't.

Step 1: Find Out How They Get Paid

Despite the seeming complexity of compensation set-ups, "financial consultants" can get paid in only two ways: commissions and fees. To understand this distinction, think about traditional life insurance agents. Normally they work for an insurance broker (called a General Agent) and they're paid a commission only when you buy a policy.

It makes no difference how much work they do for you; if they don't sell you a policy, they don't get paid. So naturally they have a strong incentive to generate a transaction.

Now suppose you thought you needed life insurance, but you didn't want to deal with agents. You could hire an independent, fee-based consultant who would help you determine if you needed coverage based on your situation. If you did, he would help you determine the type of policy that was most appropriate for you and which company offered the best value. For this service you would pay a fee.

In the securities (stock and bond) business, the brokers are names you're familiar with: Merrill Lynch ("full-commission" broker), Charles Schwab ("discount" broker), even E-Trade (Internet-based broker). Those firms, not their employees, are really the "stockbrokers." The agents who work for them are legally termed "registered representatives," or RRs. For the most part, RRs are paid like insurance agents: they get commissions on transactions. No transaction, no income.

Anybody Can Claim to be a "Financial Consultant"

When you talk to someone whose business card says "financial consultant" or "account executive" or some other fancy-sounding title, chances are they're just a plain old RR or life insurance agent.

They're usually licensed by their state and/or the U.S. Securities and Exchange Commission (the SEC) and are getting paid with commissions. That isn't necessarily bad. But these people are human, and if they know they're going to get paid *only* if you make a transaction, what do you think they're going to advise you to do? How objective is this "consultant" going to be?

While there are many competent, capable commission-based financial advisors, the investment options they offer are limited to products that pay a commission. It's actually against the law for them to sell you something that *doesn't* generate a commission for them and their broker.

Getting back to our insurance agent analogy, suppose that after you met with the independent consultant, he pointed out you really didn't need life insurance. After all, your debts were low, your children were grown and you had substantial investments, so in essence you were self-insured.

Was the advice less valuable because he told you to do nothing? No! It was very valuable because he helped you avoid spending money on insurance you really didn't need. He collected his fee whether you made a transaction or not. You paid for good advice, not for someone to help you with a transaction.

Step 2: Find a Seasoned, Trustworthy Investment Advisor Representative

Another kind of "financial consultant" is a professional called an Investment Advisor Representative (IAR). Also licensed by the SEC or their home state, IARs act as true consultants and charge you for advice, not transactions.

As a result, the IAR is much more likely to be objective, to offer you more investment choices and to be acting with your best interests in mind, not their own. IARs work through a Registered Investment Advisor entity. This is a firm that, unlike a broker, serves its clients on a fee-for-service basis, and is not paid commissions.

As in the case of insurance consultants, sometimes the best advice your advocate can give is to do nothing. In my career, I've probably helped my clients make and save more money by advising them to sit tight than I have by advising them to make changes in their portfolios.

Human nature says if your portfolio isn't doing well, you should make changes until you find something that works. But as we'll learn in upcoming chapters, that may be the worst thing you could do! Ideally you want your advocate to have a vested interest in your success. *The better you do, the better they do.* It's a win/win situation. That's why I believe you'll be served better by an advisor who is paid by fee-for-service instead of commissions or mark-ups on transactions.

Take a moment and look at the charts on this and the following page. It reveals another important and little-known reason for choosing an IAR over an RR.

CONTRASTING FIDUCIARY STANDARDS OF CARE

Registered Representatives (RRs) Paid a Commission by a Broker

- Recommend a stock or mutual fund only after studying it sufficiently to become informed as to its nature, price, and financial prognosis.

- Carry out the customer's orders best suited to the customer's interests.

- Inform the customer of the risks involved with a security.

- Refrain from self-dealing.

- Not to misrepresent any fact material to the transaction.

- Transact business only after receiving prior authorization from the customer.

In summary, the RR owes fiduciary duty to the *broker/dealer*.

Source: Case law. 11th Circuit Court
Copyright © 1999-2005, Fiduciary 360. Reprinted with permission.

CONTRASTING FIDUCIARY STANDARDS OF CARE

**Investment Advisor Representatives (IARs) Earn a
Professional Fee**

■ Know standards, laws, and trust provisions.

■ Diversify assets to specific risk/return profile of client.

■ Prepare investment policy statement.

■ Use "prudent experts" (money managers) and document
due diligence.

■ Control and account for investment expenses.

■ Monitor activities of "prudent" experts.

■ Avoid conflicts of interest and prohibited transactions.

In summary, the IAR owes fiduciary duty to the *client*.

Source: ERISA, UPIA, MPERS and related case law and regulatory opinion letters
Copyright © 1999-2005, Fiduciary 360. Reprinted with permission.

This comparison highlights the responsibilities of a typical commissioned registered representative. Notice the summary statement at the bottom. **_The RR owes his fiduciary duty to the broker/dealer._** Generally, an RR is an employee, and therefore owes his primary allegiance to the employer, not you, the client.

Now look at the IAR summary. **_The IAR owes fiduciary duty to the client._** Interesting, isn't it? Please understand; I'm not suggesting that just because someone is an IAR they can do no wrong. Far from it!

There are plenty of IARs who know how to take unfair advantage of their position when dealing with undiscerning clients, so this designation is no guarantee of competence, quality or professionalism. It just means that the IAR is _less likely_ to be motivated by a conflict of interest.

Step 3: Ask Around, Shop Around

What I _am_ suggesting is that human nature being what it is, you probably will be better served by choosing an advocate who has a legal obligation to look out for _your_ best interests, not those of his employer. That's what fiduciary duty is all about. Of course, the best way to find your advocate is to talk to people you know well, and whose judgment you trust. Ask them whom they work with or could recommend.

Ideally, you want someone you click with personally, so you may have to go through a couple of interviews to find the right match. This is important because if it works right, this relationship will be on-going.

You want to do business with someone you enjoy working with. I don't care how smart an advisor is or how many degrees they have. If you don't enjoy the relationship, or if the chemistry isn't right, find another advocate!

Fortunately, your advocate doesn't have to live in your neighborhood to be effective. I work with many clients whom I rarely, if ever, see in person. But with the Internet, fax machines, e-mail and UPS, I can and do serve my clients as effectively as if I lived next door. So don't limit yourself to advisors in your hometown.

Step 4: Check on Experience and Credentials

Ideally, you want your advocate to have broad financial experience and knowledge. Besides investment expertise, they should have a good working knowledge of tax and estate law, insurance benefits and retirement planning. This is important so that your investment advocate can work successfully with your other advisors, like your CPA and attorney.

Credentials are important to ensure you're working with someone who's done more than just pass a licensing exam. Unfortunately, most large brokerage firms focus the bulk of their professional development on product knowledge and sales training. So at the very least you want an advocate who's taken the initiative to earn one of the following professional designations:

- Certified Financial Planner (CFP)
- Chartered Financial Consultant (ChFC)
- Accredited Personal Financial Specialist (PFS)
- Registered Financial Planner (RFP)

You also want your advocate to have some seasoning and experience. Over the ten years from the mid-1990s to the mid-2000s, the U.S. stock market soared to record highs and sunk to gut-wrenching lows.

Your advocate should have experience working in each of these challenging market environments, and should be able to show you how their clients have benefited from their help during these market cycles. Of course, past performance is no guarantee of future results, so consider their track record as only one factor among many.

I'd suggest you want your advocate to have a minimum of ten years of actual, proven experience. Besides earning one of the professional designations listed above, it would be helpful if your advocate maintained a strong commitment to continuing education, because in the financial world, things change fast.

Advanced Training Recommended

Personally, I chose to earn my professional designation, Chartered Financial Consultant (ChFC), from the American College in Bryn Mawr, Pennsylvania. I selected the American College because of its outstanding reputation and flexible course schedule.

This was an excellent, broad-based program with practical training in income and estate taxes, retirement planning strategies, investments and insurance benefits.

Earning the ChFC designation gave me a solid footing in the basics, but as my practice matured I realized it wasn't enough. I decided to focus on enhancing my knowledge base so I could serve clients with more complex needs. Ultimately, I enrolled in the Cannon School's Wealth Management Program at Northwestern University and earned my Certified Wealth Manager® designation.

Cannon provides advanced training strategies and techniques designed to enable advisors to help very wealthy clients manage their assets. "Very wealthy" is defined as having a net worth of over $10 million.

Happily, I've realized that the same techniques I learned about helping wealthy people can work for my clients with fewer assets. So my clients don't have to be multi-millionaires to benefit from my training. In 2003 I earned my Accredited Investment Fiduciary (AIF)® designation from the Center for Fiduciary Studies at the University of Pittsburgh.

This specialized training enables me to help business owners manage their qualified retirement plans prudently and reduce their exposure to unlimited personal liability. When interviewing your advocate candidates, look for a strong commitment to on-going professional education.

Step 5: Get Straight on How Much You're Paying

What type of fee structure would be reasonable? I hate to sound like a politician, but that depends. To simplify, I'll just give you some general guidelines.

My fee schedule starts at one and a quarter percent (1.25%) of the value of assets under management, and begins to decline at various dollar levels down to 1/10 of 1% based on the size of the account. While I can't guarantee it, I feel confident that over time I should be able to easily earn as much, and possibly more than that for my clients.

You'll find that many fee-based advisors, especially those working at large brokerage firms, charge 1.5% to 2% initially. They typically have to charge more because their firms take a big chunk for overhead and profits. It was commonplace ten years ago to find advisors charging 2.5% to 3% annually. However, as more clients move from traditional commissioned brokers to fee-based advisors, there is a growing trend toward lower fee schedules.

In a corporate situation where I'm dealing with a number of partners, each with substantial assets, a quantity discount applies and my fee is lower because I'm dealing with a larger group. When you're interviewing various potential advocates, don't be shy. Ask how their fee schedule stacks up to their competitors. After all, it *is* your money.

However, you don't necessarily want to hire the advisor with the lowest fee. Generally, you do get what you pay for and some advisors may be able to deliver enough extra value to easily justify a somewhat higher fee.

Half Brain or Whole Brain?

It's probably safe to say that most of the people who enter the financial services industry are numbers-oriented. They like facts and figures, love crunching numbers and get turned on creating complex financial plans.

Psychologists label these types as "left-brain" oriented. This refers to the side of the brain that thinks logically, sequentially and is good with numbers. Left-brained people are wonderful folks, often highly intelligent and technically knowledgeable.

Trouble is, the majority of the business owners they serve are often creative, visionary types. They tend to be more interested in the big picture than in the details. Psychologists call this type "right-brain" oriented. The right hemisphere of the brain is more intuitive, creative and random-thinking.

Right-brain folks' eyes glaze over when their financial advisor starts talking about rates of return, tax brackets and sophisticated investment strategies.

My personal experience suggests business owners really aren't interested in the nuances and details of financial management. What they are interested in is free time to do what they want to do; namely, spend it with their friends and families.

"Right-brainers" want time to give back to their community, to make a positive difference in the lives of those less fortunate. They take comfort in the knowledge that they have a well-thought-out plan designed to nurture, grow and protect the income they'll need when they ultimately retire so they can enjoy their ideal lifestyle.

They want their children and grandchildren to grow up with strong moral characters and to learn universal laws of success that will serve them well throughout their lives.

This is what most business owners *really* value, not investment techniques, estate planning strategies and the like. If this rings true for you, then you want your advocate to understand the value of taking what I call the "whole-brain" approach to financial management.

Yes, your advocate needs to be smart, and understand the complex financial stuff. But they should also understand and embrace your hopes, plans and dreams and incorporate this into the advice they provide. So when you're interviewing your potential advocate, keep this in mind. You want a whole-brain advocate; not one with half a brain!

In Summary

I hope I've made my point: If you don't have the time, temperament, training or interest to manage your own retirement investments, you'll be much better off finding and hiring an investment professional to help you. Finding a knowledgeable, trustworthy advocate isn't easy, but it's worth the effort. You'll sleep better at night knowing you have a real pro helping you, someone who's on your side of the table; someone who's motivation to succeed is the same as yours.

Remember . . .

☞ You want your advocate's interests aligned with yours. Human nature being what it is, you should choose a fee-based advisor instead of a commission-based salesperson.

☞ An investment advisor representative has a legal, fiduciary obligation to put your interests first, not their firm's. However, this designation doesn't guarantee competence.

☞ Experience and training are important. Your advocate should have a minimum of ten years' experience and have earned a professional designation.

☞ Your personality should "click" with your advocate. Work with someone you like.

☞ Your advocate doesn't have to live in your town to work with you.

☞ Look for an advocate who takes a whole-brain approach to financial management.

Resource:

The U.S. Securities and Exchange Commission (SEC) has an excellent guide you may want to review: **http://www.sec.gov/investor/pubs/invadvisers.htm** "Questions for your financial advisor." This free guide will help you ask the right questions so you can find your ideal investment advocate.

SECRET #4

Don't Worry, Be Happy

How Fear, Hope and Greed Sabotage Investment Success

In this chapter you'll discover:

☞ Why many mutual fund investors earn miserably low returns.

☞ Just because stocks have been going up, down or sideways for the past few years doesn't mean that's going to continue.

☞ Why being out of the market and missing just a few of its best up-days can dramatically reduce your investment returns.

☞ Just as surgeons don't operate on family members, so should you refrain from managing your own retirement funds.

☞ Why the most sensitive nerve in your body runs from your brain to your wallet.

☞ How delegating the investment process eliminates the emotional component.

Dalbar is a financial-services market research firm in Boston that does regular studies of how investors are faring in the marketplace. According to their April 1, 2004 study[1], do-it-yourself mutual fund investors who attempt to "time" the market don't do very well at all.

Here's an excerpt from the report:

Dalbar's Quantitative Analysis of Investor Behavior.

*Examining the flows into and out of mutual funds for the last 20 years, the Dalbar study of investor behavior found that market timers in stock mutual funds lost **3.29%** per year on average. Over a period when the S&P grew by 12.98%, the average investor earned only 3.51%.*

How could this happen? How could the S&P 500 average over 12% annually and the typical mutual fund investor earn only a fraction of that? The findings support a similar Dalbar study released in 2003:

Motivated by fear and greed, investors pour money into equity funds on market upswings and are quick to sell on downturns. Most investors are unable to profitably time the market and are left with equity fund returns lower than inflation.

---

[1] http://www.dalbarinc.com/

Fear and Greed (you'll see why I include Hope in a minute), normal human emotions, are the driving forces that sabotage investment returns, according to Dalbar.

How Can So Many People Be So Wrong?

I've noticed that investors seem to think that whatever has been happening over the past few years will continue in the years to come. This is the cycle most do-it-yourself investors struggle with, and it helps to explain why they usually do so poorly. To illustrate this point, let's use the 13-year period from January 1992 through December 2004.

The data I'll be using come from *Ibbotson Analyst Version 8.6*. We'll use the S&P 500 index as our proxy for the stock market. Here are the total returns from 1992-2004 (include dividends):

1992	1993	1994	1995	1996	1997	1998	1999
7.67	9.99	1.31	37.43	23.07	33.36	28.58	21.04

2000	2001	2002	2003	2004
-9.11	**-11.88**	**-22.10**	28.7	10.87

Obviously, 1992 through 1994 weren't great years for stocks. Fear influenced investors to underweight stocks because the stock market wasn't doing well. Then in 1995, the stock market began an unprecedented five-year surge, with stocks up over 20% annually! Investors *Hoped* the rally would continue.

Fear, Hope, now Greed

In the late 1990's, *Greed* set in and many investors convinced themselves that a "new era" had dawned for stocks. All the old rules of prudent investing didn't apply any more, they thought. Millions of investors, fueled by *Greed*, threw caution to the wind and invested their retirement plans 100% in aggressive stocks.

The angst over Y2K (remember that?) proved to be unfounded as we moved into the new millennium. But in the spring of 2000, cracks began to show in the stock market. Unfortunately, old man *Greed* was in full control and most investors chose to *Hope* that the minus **9.11%** return for 2000 was just a little breather and 2001 would bring another big upsurge for stocks.

But 2001 brought more of the same bad news, and the market ended down **11.88%**. TV pundits suggested that surely 2002 would be a good year because stocks hadn't suffered three negative years in a row since the 1930's. Investors *Hoped* they were right and hung on. Besides, they couldn't sell stocks now because they were down over 21% from the market highs. Better to wait for the market to recover and then they would diversify their portfolios.

Well, in 2002 the market saw its biggest one-year decline in a quarter-century, losing over **22%** of its value. Now, *Fear* gripped investors again. Many had lost half or more of their portfolios, but evidently thought it was better to sell now and save what they could than suffer through another year like this. Fearing more losses, they sold their stocks and put their money in bonds or low-yielding guaranteed accounts.

And guess what happened: stocks rebounded once again in 2003, gaining over 28%! But the investors, traumatized and paralyzed by *Fear*, sat on the sidelines and watched it happen without benefiting from it. Fear, Hope and Greed, normal human emotions, apparently wrecked the financial dreams of untold numbers of retirement plan investors.

Why Timing the Market Doesn't Work

I'd like to share a thought-provoking report I saw about the importance of sticking with your investment strategy instead of trying to time the market's ups and downs. This report, provided by the AIM Family of Mutual Funds, reveals what would have happened if you missed the one day (that's right *one* day) every year when the market had its best performance.

This report covers a ten-year period from December 31, 1993 through December 31, 2003. If you had been in the market the entire year, but happened to be out of it during the *one best day* each year, your returns would have dropped by almost 50%! Missing the *two best days* each year would have dropped your returns by over 80%!

With this information, the Dalbar study we looked at earlier starts to make more sense. Instead of setting and keeping to an investment strategy based on buying and holding a well-diversified portfolio, investors try to "beat" the market by guessing when it will go up and down. So they jump in and out, driven by the Fear, Greed and Hope generated by yesterday's headlines.

Even if they jumped out of the market at precisely the right moment, but then did not get back in fast enough to catch the one best day of the year, they paid a steep price. Here's a reproduction of part of the AIM Funds report:

Some investors like to wait for just the right moment to get into the stock market... and for just the right time to pull their investment out. If that sounds like you, there's something you should know. While you're sitting on the sidelines, some of the market's best single-day performances could slip right past you.

Are you so confident in your timing strategy that you're willing to forfeit those gains? Missing even a handful of them could cost you dearly.

Missing the 20 best days could affect your
returns considerably

If you had invested $10,000 in the S&P 500 Index on December 31, 1993, by December 31, 2003, your $10,000 would have grown to $28,549, an average annual total return of 11.06%.

But suppose during that 10-year period there were times when you decided to get out of the market and, as a result, you missed the market's 10 best single-day performances. In that case, your 11.06% return would have fallen to 5.93%. If you had missed the market's 20 best days, that 11.06% return would have dropped to 2.05%. Of course, past performance cannot guarantee comparable future results.

The Penalty for Missing the Market

Trying to time the market can be an inexact—and costly—exercise. This chart represents a $10,000 investment in the S&P 500 Index from Dec. 31, 1993-Dec. 31, 2003.

Period of Investment	Average Annual Total Return	Growth of $10,000
Fully Invested	11.06%	$28,549
Miss the 10 Best Days	5.93	17,785
Miss the 20 Best Days	2.05	12,247
Miss the 30 Best Days	-1.29	8,785
Miss the 40 Best Days	-4.06	6,604
Miss the 60 Best Days	-8.74	4,009

Source: FactSet Research Systems Inc.
The S&P 500 Index is an unmanaged index considered representative of the U.S. stock market. Performance reflects reinvestment of dividends. An investment cannot be made directly in an index. This information is for illustrative purposes only and does not reflect the performance of any AIM fund.

Emotions are part of being human, and I wouldn't want it any other way. Where would we be without love and joy, excitement and expectation? Emotions give life its drama: comedy, tragedy and everything in between. But emotions should not be a component of your investment decision-making process.

This is the reason surgeons don't operate on their own family members, even if they are highly qualified to do so. The emotional component could interfere with their judgment, and lead to disastrous results. For the very same reason, you should delegate the management of your retirement funds to a qualified, trustworthy advocate.

I've heard it said that the most sensitive nerve in a person's body runs from their brain to their wallet. That might explain why emotions wreak such havoc when you're trying to make prudent investment decisions. And that's why delegating this task to an objective, seasoned investment advocate, who's experienced the usual ups and downs of the market, makes sense for the vast majority of business owners.

Remember . . .

☞ Most mutual fund investors earn miserably low returns because of the emotions of fear, hope and greed.

☞ The investment climate will change. Just because stocks have been going up, down or sideways for the past few years doesn't mean that's going to continue.

☞ Being out of the market and missing just a few of its best up-days can dramatically reduce your investment returns.

☞ Just as highly qualified surgeons don't operate on family members because emotions can cloud their judgment, so should you refrain from managing your retirement funds.

☞ The most sensitive nerve in your body runs from your brain to your wallet.

☞ Delegating the investment process substantially reduces the emotional component.

Resource:

If you had $50,000 in 1932 and invested $10,000 in the five stocks of the Dow Jones you felt were the best bets, how would you have done knowing what you do about history? Go to my website **retirerich-online.com** and click on the **"Rich"** link. Then click on the **"Stock Picking"** link and take the **Investment Quiz**.

SECRET #5

Your Money Map

An Investment Policy Statement Can Be The Key to Your Success

In this chapter you'll discover:

☞ Why an Investment Policy Statement is a powerful tool to keep you focused on your investment objective.

☞ The process your advocate will use to accomplish your goal.

☞ Why wealthy families and institutions use an IPS, and why you should too.

☞ How an IPS helps to factor out the emotions that can sabotage you.

☞ Why you should review your IPS with your advocate regularly.

☞ That an IPS can't guarantee investment success, but using one gives you a much greater probability of meeting your goals.

As a successful business owner, you understand the value of taking the time to develop and follow a well-thought-out business plan. A well-written business plan serves as a road map to guide you on the path to achievement and success. It helps keep you focused on your most important goals so you don't get sidetracked by all the day-to-day crises that constantly demand your attention.

For the same reasons, your retirement funds need a written plan too. Such a plan is known as an Investment Policy Statement (IPS). These statements have been used by wealthy families, pension plans, endowments and foundations for many years.[1] In fact IPSs are considered so important, that since the passage of the Employee Retirement Income Security Act (ERISA) in 1974, Congress requires businesses that sponsor a qualified retirement plan, like a 401(k), pension or profit sharing plan, to document their investment process with an IPS.[2]

You are not required to have an IPS for your personal retirement funds. But if some of the wealthiest people in the world understand the value of having an IPS, and if Congress requires fiduciaries for qualified retirement plans to use them, then maybe you should have one too.

---

[1] http://www.fi360.com/
[2] http://www.dol.gov/ebsa/

What an IPS Looks Like, and Why It's So Important

If you've never seen a well-drafted Investment Policy Statement, you're probably wondering what one looks like. You can see a sample in Appendix C, but for now let's focus on why an IPS is so important. In their ground-breaking work, *Prudent Investment Practices; a Handbook for Investment Fiduciaries,*[1] the Foundation for Fiduciary Studies writes:

> *Practice No 3.1: There is detail to implement a specific investment strategy*
>
> *The preparation and maintenance of the investment policy statement ("IPS") is one of the most critical functions of the fiduciary. The IPS should be viewed as the business plan and the essential management tool for directing and communicating the activities of the portfolio. It is a formal, long-range, strategic plan that allows the fiduciary to coordinate the management of the investment program in a logical and consistent framework. All material investment facts, assumptions, and opinions should be included.*
>
> *The IPS should have sufficient detail that a third party would be able to implement the investment strategy; be flexible enough that it can be implemented in a complex and dynamic financial environment; and yet not be so detailed it requires constant revisions and updates. The IPS should combine elements of planning and philosophy...*
>
> *Addendums should be used to identify information that will change on a more frequent basis such as the names of board members, accountant, attorney, actuary and money managers/mutual funds; and the capital markets assumptions used to develop the plan's asset allocation.*

Your Money Map

Your Investment Policy Statement is a written description of your primary financial goals and may include additional sub-goals. It will provide a time frame to accomplish the goal(s) and will describe how the funds will be invested.

It will identify a target return and may show you how a similarly-invested portfolio has performed over various time periods. This helps you understand how the markets have fluctuated over time.

[1] http://www.cfstudies.com/

And while past performance is no guarantee of future results, you'll have a good idea of how your funds may fluctuate in the future.

Your IPS will describe the investment strategy your advocate intends to use to accomplish your goals and how the funds may be re-balanced over time. It will describe the types of investment vehicles (stocks, bonds, mutual funds) that will be allowed and any investment products or strategies to be avoided.

Criteria will be established spelling out why, how and when an investment manager would be changed. Finally, your advocate will ask you to sign your IPS and keep a copy in your file. At that point, you will have a written document that clearly outlines what you're trying to accomplish. Instead of attempting to find "hot" investments, your advocate will be working to help you use a proven process to accomplish your goals.

As your advocate monitors your portfolio, he'll be reporting how you're doing. An IPS helps you answer the question "How am I doing relative to my goals?" It also helps you realistically judge the value of your advocate's help.

The Power of Your Investment Policy Statement

As we saw in Secret #4, normal human emotions like Fear, Hope and Greed often conspire to destroy a well-thought-out investment strategy. Your IPS will serve as a buffer to help you drain away the emotions that well up during scary market events. *Such events could drive you to make precisely the wrong move at the wrong time.*

You may remember I mentioned (in Secret #3) how important it is for me to advise clients to do nothing at times. Well, in November of 2002 I got a call from a client (I'll call him Tom) who'd been with me only since February of that year. He was worried because his account was down a few percent, and wondered if he should pull out of his stock funds altogether until things turned around. Sound familiar? Have you ever felt such an urge after reading the morning stock reports?

Mr. Fear had been working overtime on poor Tom's psyche—and no wonder! You'll recall that 2002 was a particularly nasty year for stocks, with the S&P 500 down more than **22%**. He'd been used to managing his own retirement funds when stocks were going up, but had hired me so he could retire and focus his time and energy on his 250-acre "gentleman's farm" in rural Virginia.

I reminded him that we'd spent considerable time discussing his goals, objectives and ideal retirement lifestyle. Then I pointed out that while we were hoping to achieve a reasonable return over time, we agreed there would be challenging periods when his account would probably earn less, or even turn negative for a while.

"Does This Still Make Sense to You?"

After reviewing his IPS with him on the phone, I noted that although his account was down a little, his IPS specifically stated this was normal and not a valid reason to change the plan. I reviewed with him the rationale I'd used to create his recommended portfolio, and asked him if it still made sense to him.

He agreed it did, and apologized for bothering me. I told him answering questions was part of my job and that we should stay the course because he had a well-thought-out plan and excellent money managers. He just needed to give it time to work for his benefit.

If we hadn't had an IPS reminding Tom why we were investing the way we were, and that down markets were a normal event, it's possible Mr. Fear would have won the day. The result would have been that Tom would have made the wrong move at the wrong time. The IPS served to drain out the emotions and enable him to assess his situation rationally.

Patience Pays Off

Now, let's fast-forward almost two years—from the date Tom first signed up with me to December 31, 2004. While past performance is no guarantee of future results, according to Raymond James portfolio performance, Tom has enjoyed a total return, after all fees, of over 30%. Compare that to the S&P 500 index, which earned less than 15% over the same time period, and you can see how staying the course paid off.

That's the power of a well-thought-out IPS. It helps to counteract the normal human emotions of Fear, Hope and Greed, which destroy so many investment plans.

Ideally, you'll want to review your IPS:
— at least annually, and
— if you're changing professional advisors, or
— experiencing a life-changing event like retirement, divorce or relocation, or
— a financial "event" like coming into a substantial inheritance or taking a large capital gain.

An IPS can't guarantee you'll achieve all your financial goals. But like a good business plan, it can help keep you focused on what's most important so you're less likely to get sidetracked by emotions, investment fads, hot tips and other temptations. When you're checking out potential investment advocates, ask to see a few sample IPSs. If properly prepared, they should differ based on the particular goals and retirement lifestyles identified during the initial consultations.

Regardless of your financial situation, or how much you have to invest, you can benefit from the planning and foresight that go into creating an IPS—to preserve, grow and protect your retirement money.

Remember . . .

☞ Your IPS is a powerful tool to keep you focused on your investment objective and the process your advocate will use to accomplish that objective.

☞ Wealthy families and institutions use them, and so should you.

☞ An IPS can help to factor out the emotions that can cause you to make the wrong move at the wrong time.

☞ An IPS can't guarantee investment success, but using one gives you a much greater probability of meeting your goals.

Resource:

To see different types of IPSs, go to **retirerich-online.com,** click on the **Rich** link, then click on the **Money Map** link.

SECRET #6

Your Momma Was Right

*Don't Put All Your Eggs in One Basket—And Make Sure
They're the Right Eggs*

Modern Portfolio Theory Explained

In this chapter you'll discover:

☞ Why you shouldn't gamble with your retirement money.

☞ How diversifying into different types of investments could reduce your risk.

☞ Why the kinds of investments you use and their percentages will impact your results.

☞ Why it's important to focus on the total return of your overall portfolio.

☞ Why some of your asset classes may be temporarily out-of-favor and performing poorly. And why this is normal and occasionally occurs in a properly diversified portfolio.

In November 1999 I received a phone call from a gentleman (I'll call him Sid) who told me he was ready to retire and wanted me to help him manage his retirement money. As usual, I began asking a series of questions to determine if we should schedule a personal visit or if I should refer him to another advisor.

During the course of the conversation, I learned that Sid worked for Lucent Technologies and had accumulated almost one million dollars in his 401(k) plan. He was in his mid 50's, married, and his wife did not work outside the home. Since his 401(k) had grown so rapidly, it looked like he was going to be able to retire much sooner than he ever expected.

When I asked how his money was invested now, Sid said, "I have 100% of my 401(k) in Lucent Technologies stock. It's doing great! The price is over $60 per share and I started buying at $5!" Mr. Greed had been working overtime on this poor soul. I asked him if he thought it was wise to have all his retirement money in a single stock.

He seemed surprised I would ask such a question. "This stuff's been going up like crazy, and a bunch of analysts think it'll easily hit $100 per share in the next six months. That'll almost double my money!"

I Can't Help You

As gently as I could, I explained to Sid that I couldn't help him if he wanted to keep all his money in a single stock. The risk to his financial health (and my reputation) was too great. I only work with clients who listen to their wise Mommas' advice and recognize the value of not putting all their eggs in one basket.

I didn't try to convince him I was right and he was wrong. I'd learned over the years that when Mr. Greed is in charge, no one can disagree with him.

I suggested that if he planned to keep all his money in that one stock, Sid should just open up an IRA brokerage account on-line and roll his funds into that. He wouldn't need an investment advisor to implement this "non-strategy."

Eventually, curiosity got the better of me and I asked him why he wanted to hire me and pay my fee if he just planned to hold Lucent stock. He replied: "Well, my wife doesn't know anything about managing money, and if anything happened to me I want her to have someone she can trust to take care of this for her."

What a nice guy, I thought, caring about his wife like that! Unfortunately, Mr. Greed had blinded him to the incredible risk he was taking with his and his wife's financial future. He couldn't understand why I refused to work with him.

Sid told me he had talked to a couple of stockbrokers in town and they were eager to get his account. But he'd called me because a business-owner friend he highly respected had recommended me. Despite being told by a valued friend to take my advice, he refused to consider selling even part of his Lucent stock as a way of spreading his risk.

Since we were at an impasse, I thanked him for his consideration and wished him well. Soon I pretty much forgot about our conversation, and I never heard from him again.

Three Years Later

In 2002 I happened to be reviewing some stock reports and came across Lucent Technologies. It was trading for less than 60 CENTS per share! The chart that follows shows the market activity of Lucent Technologies

Lucent Technologies - LU

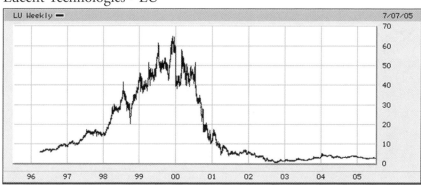

Source: BigCharts.com

stock from 1996, when it was introduced, through late 2005. Notice the price was right around $60 when I talked with Sid, and indeed, it did go up later in the year—not to $100, but to just $63.57.

The lowest price traded was 55 cents. Though it later recovered slightly (to $5). But at 60 cents a share, his million-dollar "portfolio" would be worth a bit less than $10,000.

Now, I don't know if Sid ever did the right thing and diversified his money. But knowing what we do about human nature from Secret #4, the odds are Mr. Greed kept telling him to hang on, and cost him virtually his entire retirement nest-egg. If so, he and his wife will have to live with his poor investment decision for the rest of their lives.

Which Eggs Do You Choose for *Your* Investment Basket?

You don't have to be a genius to know it's a good idea to avoid putting all your investment eggs in one basket. Your Momma knew it. There's even a technical name for it: "diversification." And while it might seem like plain old common sense, three renowned mathematicians, Harry Markowitz, William Sharpe and Merton Miller shared a Nobel Prize in 1990 for proving that diversification works![1]

The even-more-impressive name they came up with for not putting all your eggs in one basket is "Modern Portfolio Theory" (MPT)[2].

1 http://nobelprize.org/economics/laureates/1990/
2 ibid

But here's the secret they discovered that may not be so obvious. The *eggs* (types of investments) you choose for your basket (total investment portfolio), and the percentage each one makes up in the overall portfolio can have a huge impact on your ultimate results.

Their research revealed that it was important to have a variety of different types of investments working together in order to lower a portfolio's risk of loss and improve its chances of generating reasonable returns over time.

They discovered that different types of investments move in and out of favor, depending on various market conditions. And since nobody knew which asset classes (stocks, bonds, real estate, international stocks, foreign bonds, etc.) would perform well in the future, it was important to build a portfolio with holdings in a variety of different investments.

Now, most amateur investors think they can jump from one hot investment to another and make money that way. The problem is they don't know what's hot until *after* it's gone up a lot. So by getting in *after* the big upswing, they're usually buying at the top, just before it begins to go back down. The key is to have money invested in holdings that may be out of favor right now, but ultimately should move back into favor over time.

Building Your Portfolio

The table on page 52 lists six different types of financial asset classes. Look across the top at the different headings. The first is **U.S. Long-Term Corporate Bonds**, and here's how they work. For illustrative purposes only, let's use a large well-known company like DuPont. Suppose DuPont needs some money to modernize its plants to make them more competitive. They choose to sell bonds in order to raise the needed cash.

If you buy a bond, in exchange for your money DuPont gives you a certificate that states how much they're going to pay in interest (yield), which is usually fixed and paid every six months, and how many years before they'll give you your money back (maturity).

If everything goes according to plan, you'll earn the stated interest every year. And if DuPont stays in good financial health, you'll get your money back. With long-term bonds you usually get your money back in 20 years or so. In essence, you're renting your money to DuPont in exchange for regular interest payments.

The **S&P 500** is a stock index made up of the 500 biggest companies in America. If you buy stocks, you'll receive a certificate stating the number of shares you own. When you own stock you are a part owner in the underlying company. If the company pays out part of their profits in the form of dividends, you'll get a check generally every 90 days.

If the company does well, the value of your stock will increase. If the company doesn't do well, the stock can decline. Unlike with bonds, there is no guarantee you'll ever get your money back when you buy stocks. The companies' size is calculated by multiplying the number of shares of stock that have been sold (shares outstanding) by the current share price. This is known as the capitalization rate or "cap" for short. Companies in the S&P 500 are known as **Large-Cap** companies.

Next is **U. S. Small Stock** and **S&P Mid-Cap 400**, which are indexes like the S&P 500. The big difference is the size of these companies, since they have capitalizations much smaller than the S&P 500. U.S. small stocks are called **Small-Cap** and medium-sized companies are called **Mid-Cap**.

The formula used to determine which stocks are considered large, medium and small varies over time and is beyond the scope of this book. See the *Wall St. Journal Guide to Money and Investing* for more detailed information about cap rates.

Next we have **NAREIT Equity,** which is the National Association of Real Estate Investment Trusts. These are stocks comprised of various real estate holdings and they usually pay attractive dividends because of the cash flow generated by many real estate investments.

Finally we have **MSCI-EAFE,** which stands for Morgan Stanley Capital International-Europe, Australia, Far East. This too is a stock index comprised of companies outside the US. These are just a few of the indexes available in the investment world.

Now, focus on the numbers in the following chart for every year in **bold**. These are investments with the highest total returns (Dividends + Share Price Gains or Losses + Interest) for that particular year. Do you notice any patterns? That's right; ***there are no patterns!*** Some years an asset class will be at or near the top. Other years it's at or near the bottom. In still other years it may be anywhere in between.

	U.S. LT Corp Bonds	S&P 500	U.S. Small Stock	S&P Mid-Cap 400	NAREIT-Equity	MSCI EAFE
Dec-90	**6.78**	-3.17	-21.56	-5.12	-15.35	-23.19
Dec-91	19.89	30.55	44.63	**50.10**	35.70	12.49
Dec-92	9.39	7.67	**23.35**	11.91	14.59	-11.85
Dec-93	13.19	9.99	20.98	13.96	19.65	**32.95**
Dec-94	-5.76	1.31	3.11	-3.57	3.17	**8.06**
Dec-95	27.20	**37.43**	34.46	30.94	15.27	11.55
Dec-96	1.40	23.07	17.62	19.20	**35.26**	6.36
Dec-97	12.95	**33.36**	22.78	32.26	20.29	2.06
Dec-98	10.76	**28.58**	-7.31	19.12	-17.51	20.33
Dec-99	-7.45	21.04	**29.79**	14.72	-4.62	27.30
Dec-00	12.87	-9.11	-3.59	17.51	**26.36**	-13.96
Dec-01	10.65	-11.88	**22.77**	-0.61	13.93	-21.21
Dec-02	**16.33**	-22.10	-13.28	-14.51	3.81	-15.66
Dec-03	5.27	28.70	**60.70**	35.61	37.14	39.17
Dec-04	8.72	10.87	18.39	16.48	**31.58**	20.70
5 Yr.	10.77	-0.71	17.00	10.90	22.57	1.81
10 Yr.	9.87	14.00	18.23	17.07	16.15	7.66
15 Yr.	9.48	12.42	16.86	15.87	14.62	6.34

Includes index growth and reinvestment of any dividends & income where applicable.
Source: Ibbotson Analyst Version 8.6 ©2004. *This report is not indicative of any security's performance and is based on information believed reliable. Future performance cannot be guaranteed and investment yields will fluctuate with market conditions. Index total returns also do not reflect taxes, commissions or management fees. Past performance is not indicative of future results.*

	U.S. LT Corp Bonds	S&P 500	U.S. Small Stock	S&P Mid-Cap 400	NAREIT-Equity	MSCI EAFE
Years as Best Performer	2	3	4	1	3	2

Make A Note: This Is Important!

The trick is to build a portfolio using enough different types of investments so that, on balance, you'll always have *something* that's performing well.

The flip side to this is *some* of your holdings will probably be performing poorly. But that's OK because it's the *total return* (sum of all your investments) you're interested in, not how each is doing individually. I recently wrote a magazine article in which I highlighted the critical value of prudent diversification for a retirement portfolio. As an example, I used the case of three hypothetical investors. Here's part of that article:

A Tale of Three Investors

Let's look at three hypothetical 401(k) investors and go back to November 1, 1999. They're all age 50, have $500,000 in their accounts, and are adding $10,000 every year.

Investor #1 has been reading financial magazines and is convinced technology is the place to put his money. So he invests everything in the NASDAQ stock index, loaded with technology and other start-up companies. Two months after he made this move he's up over 30% and he's thrilled! At this rate he figures he can retire late next year.

Investor #2 also reads financial magazines and watches nightly business reports. He's more conservative and figures if he stays with the "big companies" he'll be OK. So he puts everything in the S&P 500 stock index, which is comprised of the 500 biggest companies in America. By the end of two months he's up almost 10%. He figures he can retire in three years.

Investor #3 hires an advisor who develops a disciplined investment strategy for him using Asset Allocation (a fancy term for not putting all your eggs in one basket). He divides his money among stock funds of large, medium and small companies, adding in some foreign funds and real estate funds. He tops it all off with some government bond funds for stability.

The advisor explains that every quarter, the portfolio will be re-balanced to take advantage of normal market fluctuations. The advisor charges an annual fee of 1/2 of 1% of the portfolio's value. After two months, Investor #3 is up a little over 5%. After hearing his buddies bragging in the break room about how well they're doing, he's wondering if he'd made the right decision.

Fast-forward five years. On October 31, 2004, here's how they did, according to Morningstar Mutual Funds. Remember they all started out with $500,000 and added $10,000 per year.

	Ending Value	Percent Gain(Loss)	Gain(Loss)
Investor #1	$382,401	(36.8%)	($167,599)
Investor #2	$502,648	(9.35%)	($47,352)
Investor #3	$774,472	**+36.95%***	**+$224,472***

*Net return to the investor after all fees and expenses deducted.

Mind you, this is completely hypothetical. Past performance is no guarantee of future results and hiring a professional investment advisor may not improve your performance. But back in late 1999, with the stock market soaring and the popular financial press cheering it on, only a minority of 401(k) participants had the dis-cipline to buck the trend and stick with an appropriately-diversi-fied portfolio. (See appendix B for complete article.)

Developing your Personal Retirement Portfolio

In order to create a retirement investment portfolio, you'll probably need to meet with your investment advocate several times. Don't hold anything back. Tell them what you're really thinking, feeling and hoping for. It's the only way they'll know enough about your unique situation to help you.

Yes, it will take more time, energy and patience to do this, but the results are exponentially superior. I've found that one of the most valuable conversation starters with a client is, "Tell me about yourself." Then I sit back and take notes. People love to talk about themselves, and once I get the pump primed, the words start flowing!

Often, after I've met with clients and had this conversation, I'll call them back to get the answers to questions I may have thought of later. It will probably take your advocate a few weeks to develop your portfolio, document it in your Investment Policy Statement (see Secret #5) and then meet with you to review it for your approval.

How Would You Like To Proceed?

At the conclusion of this meeting, you get to decide how you want to proceed. You may want to take everything home and mull it over before you do anything. That's perfectly fine. A truly professional advocate will not push you to do something you're not ready for. If you need a week or so to digest things, by all means take it.

My experience with successful business owners has been that they know how to make decisions. As someone who makes decisions all the time, if you're comfortable, you'll be ready to get moving. However, your spouse may need some more time. If this is the case, take a little more time and keep the peace at home.

You always knew it made sense to avoid putting all your eggs in one basket. Didn't your Momma tell you that? Mine did. Now you know why, and how it's done to build a retirement investment portfolio designed to stand up to normal market fluctuations. "Modern Portfolio Theory" can't guarantee you'll always earn a good return on your retirement funds, but it's a proven strategy used by the wealthiest people and largest financial institutions in the world. Shouldn't you take your cue from them and use it too?

Remember . . .

☞ Don't gamble with your retirement money. The stakes are too high.

☞ By diversifying into different types of investments, you should reduce your risk.

☞ The kinds of investments you use and their percentages will impact your results.

☞ Focus on the total return of your overall portfolio, not on individual holdings.

☞ Some of your asset classes may be temporarily out-of-favor and performing poorly. This is normal and occasionally occurs in a properly diversified portfolio.

Resource:

For a more complete listing of how various investments have performed over the years, go to **retirerich-online.com,** click on the **Rich** link, then click on **Asset Class Returns.**

SECRET #7

"Look Ma, No Hands!"

*Passive vs. Active Money Management:
The Great Indexing Dilemma.*

In this chapter you'll discover:

☞ The popular financial press would have you believe index funds are always better.

☞ Historically index funds perform well in up markets, but under-perform otherwise.

☞ Based on historical market cycles, it appears we may once again be in a weak market for the foreseeable future, which would suggest actively-managed funds may outperform.

☞ Index funds under-perform in weak markets because they have to hold all the stocks in their universe, including the obvious dogs.

☞ Index funds and actively managed mutual funds are both reasonable investment choices depending on market cycles and your particular circumstances.

"And now for a look at today's business news. Stocks finished higher, with the Dow Jones Industrial Average gaining 32 points while the S&P 500 rose 7 points."

Unless you've been living in Tibet, you've probably heard newscasts like this as long as you can remember. But do you really know what stock indexes are and what they mean? For the moment, I'll assume you don't and give you a quick overview.

The Dow Jones Industrials Average (DJIA) is the aggregate value of the stocks of 30 of the largest companies in the United States. The number you hear quoted on the radio or TV is based on a calculation that was devised many years ago and is recalculated every time a change is made.

The stocks chosen for this index supposedly represent a cross-section of American industry. And though they are called "industrials," some of them, like McDonald's, aren't industrial at all. AT&T was part of the index for many years (even though it wasn't technically an "industrial" either), but was recently removed because that company doesn't hold the dominant position in the economy that it used to.

Many market analysts ignore the DJIA because they feel that, with such a small number of stocks, the index doesn't really reflect what's going on in a gigantic and widely diverse marketplace.

A Broader Measure

The S&P 500 is an index made up of the stocks of the 500 largest U.S. companies, as determined by an organization called Standard & Poor's (S&P). Since it's a broader measure, market professionals pay more attention to the S&P 500 than the DJIA.

Of course there are many other indexes like the Russell 2000, the MSCI EAFE, and the NASDAQ. The NASDAQ has come into prominence in recent years because it contains stocks of many high-tech start-up companies, the darlings of the great market boom of the late 1990's.

All indexes are helpful sources of information, but for our purposes, we're going to focus on the unmanaged S&P 500 index. The popular financial press, self-appointed consumer advocates and others who distrust the securities industry, have argued that investors should just put their money in funds that track an index, like the S&P 500. These funds simply invest in the companies that make up the index.

They say that over time, these "passive" mutual funds will beat the vast majority of funds that have a manager making hands-on, day-to-day buy and sell decisions—so-called "active" management. I've read articles claiming that the S&P 500 index all by itself outperforms 75%, 83%, even 95% of managed mutual funds.

Here's what Smart Money[1] magazine's website had to say about index funds:

> You can save yourself a whole lot of trouble and just about guarantee success by simply choosing an index fund and holding on to it for the long haul.

> Index funds are cheap. They're tax-efficient. And they routinely beat the majority of actively managed funds. Over the past 10 years, only 30% of domestic equity funds beat the S&P 500. And over the past 20 years, only slightly more than 12% did, according

---

[1] http://www.smartmoney.com/

to investment-research firm Lipper. What are the chances that you would have picked one of the few winners? Remote.

Not to be outdone, the Motley Fool[1] website had this to say:

What's Wrong With Mutual Funds?

Buy an index fund. Approximately 80% of mutual funds under-perform the average return of the stock market.

The price of "active management"

Though you'd think mutual funds provide benefits to shareholders by hiring "expert" stock pickers, the sad truth of the matter is that over time, the vast majority—approximately 80%—of mutual funds under-perform the average return of the stock market.

Markets Move in Cycles

The writers go on to suggest that you're a sap for paying someone to help you invest because any idiot can do better on their own by just buying an index fund. Of course this totally ignores the role human emotions (Greed, Fear, etc.) play in undermining our best-laid plans. But I digress.

The fact is, the people who tell you to just buy unmanaged index funds are partially right in some ways, and completely wrong in others. Yes, it's true that *on average* the S&P 500 index will outperform the majority of similarly-invested, actively-managed mutual funds *over select time periods*. In short, when the market's consistently going up (a bull market), you'll probably do fine by investing in an index fund because most stocks are rising.

However, according to Towers Data[2] research, when stocks are going down (a bear market) or stagnant, you would probably do better if you were invested in the *average* actively-managed mutual fund. Look at the following graph:

---

[1] http://www.fool.com/
[2] http://www.towersdata.com/TowersData/

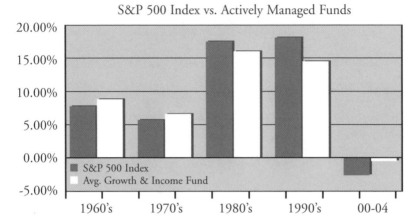

Nobody can consistently say where the market's going in the future. But we do know that historically the stock market tends to move in up-and-down cycles, with the long-term trend being up. Over the 50 years ending December 31, 2004, the S&P 500 index enjoyed an average annual return of 10.92%.[1]

As you can see, the '60s and '70s were decades when the S&P 500 Index earned *less than the average actively-managed growth & income mutual fund.* Obviously, some mutual funds *did much better* than the average, while others did worse.

But during the bull market of the '80s and '90s, this trend reversed as stocks soared to unprecedented highs, with the S&P 500 index easily beating the *average* mutual fund! Again, some funds did better than the S&P 500 while others did worse.

Now it appears a new trend has begun, with the first five years of the 2000s showing the S&P 500 index badly trailing the *average* growth & income mutual fund. Is this the start of a new challenging period for stocks like we saw in the '60s and '70s? Nobody knows for sure, but I think it might be.

Here's what Raymond James stock analyst Jeffrey Saut said in his February 14, 2005 comments:

> *...while I think over the long term stocks (in the aggregate) will outperform most other asset classes, history suggests there can be*

---

[1] http://www.towersdata.com/TowersData/

*long periods of time when the major market indexes go "flat" —
the 1965 to 1982 time frame immediately comes to mind. For an
"index investor," 1965 to 1982 was a nightmare, producing
almost NO capital gains. For the past three years, we have suggested that such an environment for the major market indices is likely
for the foreseeable future...*

Average? Why Would You Use Average Money Managers?

If you go back and read the quotes from *SmartMoney* and *Motley
Fool*, you'll notice they compare index funds' performance relative to
the average mutual fund.

An experienced, professional investment advocate will be more likely
to choose superior, proven money managers for your portfolio who've
experienced challenging markets in the past and still managed to
perform well.

Of course, past performance is no guarantee of future results, but
there are seasoned managers who have handily beaten the indexes for
decades! That's who you want working for you.

You may be wondering how much of a difference *outstanding* money
managers make compared to a similar portfolio invested solely in
average mutual funds? In a moment I'll show you an example. But
first, let's assume you had $400,000 in your retirement plan as of
January 31, 1999 and were adding $6,600 every quarter.

Let's further assume you were so caught up with Mr. Greed that you
had 100% of your money invested in the S&P 500 index. Heck, it
had been up over 20% every year for the past four years, so why not?
The best part was you didn't have to pay fees to some lame
investment advisor because you could do better on your own! At
least, that's what your brother-in-law said, and he reads *SmartMoney*,
so he must know.

According to Towers Data[1], here's what your results were as of
January 31, 2005—six years later. You would have invested $551,800
and your account value had grown to...

---

[1] http://www.towersdata.com/TowersData/

*"Oh no, that must be a typo! I only have $575,707 in my account! I've
earned $23,907 in six years; that's less than 1% per year! Guess the wife
will need to get a job so we can put more money away for retirement.
Besides, her stupid brother told me to do this. I always knew he was
an idiot!"*

Don't laugh. This type of scenario actually happened to lots of aging
baby boomers (and you know some of them) who thought they had
become investment geniuses during the late '90s and their future
financial security was assured. OK, I know you're not like that. You're
reading this book because you realize the value of delegating.

Average Diversified Fund Portfolio

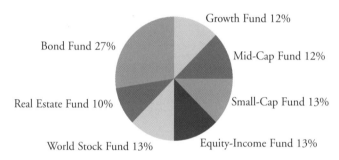

Bond Fund 27%

Growth Fund 12%

Mid-Cap Fund 12%

Small-Cap Fund 13%

Real Estate Fund 10%

World Stock Fund 13%

Equity-Income Fund 13%

A Diversified *Average* Mutual Fund Portfolio

Suppose your investment advocate wasn't particularly bright, and put
you in a diversified portfolio of *average* mutual funds. He did have
enough sense to properly diversify into different asset classes (as we
learned in Secret #6). You invested the same money at the same time
into this portfolio.

According to Towers Data[1], your account would have grown to
$733,473, a gain of $181,673. And that's after:

■ enduring the worst stock market crash since the Great Depression;

■ paying a fee to your investment advocate annually;

■ paying the mutual fund manager's fees.

[1] http://www.towersdata.com/TowersData/

You enjoyed an average annual return of 5.56%, which is nothing to brag about. But considering the circumstances, that wasn't too bad. Of course this is hypothetical, and past performance is no guarantee of future results.

The Difference Superior Fund Managers Make

Let's assume your investment advocate helped you identify and invest with some of the top mutual fund managers in this diversified portfolio.

According to Morningstar Advisor.com[1], your account would have grown to $912,202. This is a gain of $360,402— an average annual return of 9.97%. And remember, this was after:

■ enduring the worst stock market crash since the Great Depression;

■ paying your investment advocate an annual fee;

■ paying the mutual fund money manager's fees.

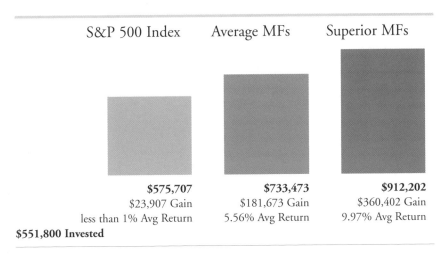

	S&P 500 Index	Average MFs	Superior MFs
	$575,707	**$733,473**	**$912,202**
	$23,907 Gain	$181,673 Gain	$360,402 Gain
	less than 1% Avg Return	5.56% Avg Return	9.97% Avg Return

$551,800 Invested

In short, the difference between buying the average funds and using outstanding money managers was about $178,729. And compared to the S&P 500 Index, which was recommended by your not-so-smart brother-in-law, you would have wound up with an extra $336,495. Of course, these are hypothetical examples and past performance is no guarantee of future results.

---

1 https://advtools.morningstar.com/

Indexing vs. Stock-Picking

OK, we've been talking about mutual funds and index funds to this point because they're the types of investment options most often found in the standard retirement plan. But what if you have a 401(k) plan that allows you to invest in individual stocks in addition to mutual funds?

Well, that opens up a whole new realm of possibilities. But remember, you don't want to take unnecessary risks with your retirement funds. I wouldn't suggest you put more than 35% of your retirement plan portfolio into individual stocks because of the difficulty in properly diversifying. Buying individual stocks is more risky than buying an index or mutual fund because you don't have the benefit of many stocks working for you.

However, your investment advocate will know which stock analysts have good long-term track records. And remember, just because a large, well-known brokerage firm recommends a particular stock doesn't mean it's a good buy. Look at the following study.

Do Stock Analysts Really Add Value?

J. Randall Woolridge, Professor of Finance at Penn State University, released a detailed study in 2004 titled, "The Returns from the Recommended Stocks of Brokerage Firms."

The study, published in the *Journal of Investing*, revealed some startling facts. In short, Dr. Woolridge discovered that only a handful of brokerage firms have been able to consistently pick stocks that outperform the S&P 500 index.

Notice that only four of the ten brokerage firms referenced (40%) were able to outperform the S&P 500 index. Indeed, some of the best-known names in the industry that do lots of advertising didn't fare very well. So it appears that some stock analysts are indeed able to add value, while the majority do not.

The following chart is taken from Professor Woolridge's study.

The Performance of Brokerage Firm Stock Recommendations
1993-2002

Firm	Average Annual Return	Highest Quarterly Return	Lowest Quarterly Return	Cumulative Wealth Index	Coefficient of Determination
Raymond James	13.98	33.1	-31.1	$3,700.45	0.43
Merrill Lynch	12.84	20.5	-16.1	$3,345.92	0.78
Bear Stearns	11.68	31.3	-18.2	$3,017.71	0.79
Credit Suisse FB	10.01	28.6	-30.1	$2,595.29	0.8
A. G. Edwards	8.49	18	-21.5	$2,258.82	0.9
Goldman Sachs	7.96	31.4	-23.2	$2,151.08	0.82
Morgan Stanley	7.64	17.3	-19.3	$2,087.58	0.9
Prudential Securities	6.34	31.8	-22.1	$1,848.94	0.73
Solomon Smith Barney	4.51	26.5	-26.5	$1,554.15	0.82
Lehman Brothers	4.05	45.8	-27.6	$1,486.91	0.8
Average	8.71	28.43	-23.57	$2,404.68	0.78
S&P 500 Returns	9.35	21.3	-17.28	$2,443.46	1.00

In Summary

Index funds are fine when the market's going up, but appear to under-perform when it's going down. Why? Because the index fund must hold all the stocks in its particular universe—even the obvious dogs that are dragging down returns. However, a good money manager should recognize the dogs and avoid them, thereby enhancing portfolio performance.

The stock market moves in cycles of ups and downs. The '60s and '70s weren't so great while the '80s and '90s were way up. Now the 2000s are down, suggesting we may be in another down or flat cycle, which would mean that based on historical precedent, active managers should do better *on average* than the indexes.

Finally, it's a good idea to avoid average money managers. When you're working with an independent investment advocate, he or she will be able to help you find the seasoned, proven managers who've generated above-average results during various challenging markets. Again, past performance is no guarantee of future results, but the fact remains that some managers seem to consistently generate above-average returns.

Are actively-managed mutual funds always the way to go? No, but the same can be said of index funds. I believe there is a place in some portfolios for both, depending on a variety of factors. But to suggest that index funds are always the best investment is short-sighted and inaccurate. Balance is the key—just as it was when you pedaled down the street on your bike and yelled, "Look Ma, no hands!"

Remember . . .

☞ The popular financial press would have you believe index funds are always better than actively-managed mutual funds.

☞ Index funds perform well in strong up markets, but under-perform when stocks are declining or stagnant.

☞ Based on historical market cycles, it appears we are once again in a weak market for the foreseeable future. This suggests actively managed funds should may better.

☞ Index funds under-perform in weak markets because they have to hold all the stocks in their universe, including the obvious dogs.

☞ Index funds and actively-managed mutual funds are both reasonable investment choices depending on market cycles and your particular circumstances.

Resource:

You can read an abstract of the study by professor Woolridge by logging on to **retirerich-online.com,** click on the **Rich** link, then click on **Abstract of Dr. Woolridge's Study.**

"20 Percent a Year? Sure, No Problem!"

Reasonable Expectations Are Crucial to Investment Success

In this chapter you'll discover:

☞ Why your basic premise is vital to your ultimate success.

☞ Even world-class money managers go through slumps, but they are usually only temporary. They didn't suddenly become "stupid."

☞ While some of your money managers will occasionally under-perform, others will probably be doing exceptionally well. Focus on your total return.

☞ Reasonable expectations will help inoculate you from the deadly virus of constantly jumping from one "hot" investment to another.

☞ You and your advocate need to agree on a reasonable return at the beginning of your relationship. You can adjust it over time by amending your IPS.

My friend and mentor, Nido Qubein[1], is a modern-day success story. He came to the U.S. from Lebanon as a teenager with just $50 in his pocket; no connections, no job—he couldn't even speak English! All he had was a dream, his ambitions and willingness to work. Today he is the Chairman of Great Harvest Bread Company, the President of High Point University, a world-renowned keynote speaker, and an internationally-respected consultant to Fortune 500 companies.

Nido says that in order to be successful, you have to start with a valid premise. For example, as an immigrant he believed that if he could just get to the United States, and was willing to work hard, he could become wealthy. That premise proved to be valid. Similarly, your premise, or mind-set, is critical to your ultimate success in life.

What does this have to do with successful retirement plan investing? I believe it's crucial, because if your expectations are unrealistic, you'll constantly be jumping from one investment strategy to another, trying to achieve those unrealistic results. You won't give yourself enough time to implement and reap the benefits of a well-thought-out, well-executed plan. And time is vital to long-term investment success.

---

[1] http://www.nidoqubein.com/

World-Class Money Managers Struggle Sometimes

The fact is, the best money managers in the world under-perform from time to time. That's normal and to be expected. So if your premise is that you expect all the managers recommended by your investment advocate to be continually generating great returns, you're setting yourself up for a costly disappointment.

My experience over nearly a quarter-century in the investment field is that high-quality money managers will probably disappoint you 30% to 40% of the time. That doesn't mean they've suddenly become stupid. It usually means their investment style has temporarily fallen out of favor based on changing economic or market conditions.

That's why it's so important to have a well-diversified portfolio working for you, as we saw in Secret #6. Sure, you may have a manager or two who's underperforming. But the odds are good you'll have another manager or two who's hitting the ball out of the park!

Even the Best Go Through Their Slumps

This reminds me of an analogy that applies here. During a long baseball season, every player will go through periods where he hits well, and other times when nothing he swings at turns into a hit. These periods are called "slumps." Nobody likes them, nobody knows exactly what brings them on, and nobody can predict when they will end. How does a baseball coach deal with slumps?

Well, first of all, he realizes that he's got a whole team full of hitters, and never do they all go into a slump at once. So while one man is struggling, others are often doing better. As a team, overall, they do OK. Second, he realizes that a quality player doesn't stop being good just because he's not hitting for a while. A .300 hitter (3 hits for 10 at bats) will hit .300 over the course of the season, even if he has a bad May or a dismal August. A good coach knows it's long-term performance that counts.

In the investment world, the same thing happens. Portfolio managers have good years and bad years. But the good ones almost always stay good and over time make up for their slumps.

Occasional Manager Changes Are Normal

Of course, there will be instances when a manager will need to be replaced with a more promising management team. Even the best players get traded away. Sometimes the lead manager retires or his best and brightest analysts are hired away by another firm. Maybe they're trying to improve performance by straying outside their discipline.

The reasons for management changes are many and varied. Your investment advocate should be keeping you apprised of any under-performing managers. And since you have a well-drafted Investment Policy Statement (Secret #5), you'll know why your advocate is recommending a manager change.

By having realistic expectations, and understanding that even the best money managers have their ups and downs, you'll inoculate yourself from the novice mistake of always chasing whatever's "hot" at the moment.

What are "Realistic" Expectations?

What should you expect from your investment advocate in terms of results? As we learned in Secret #5, you should have clearly written goals and objectives that are agreed upon by you and your advocate. Ideally, your advocate should generate annual returns for you that are 1% to 2% (depending on how aggressive you want to be) higher than your agreed-upon benchmark. This is net to you, after all fees and expenses are deducted.

This may not sound like much, but over the years an extra 1% to 2%, allowed to accumulate, can make a huge difference. In addition, your investment advocate should help you reduce the amount of volatility (market ups and downs) you're subject to. This will help you sleep better at night and calm your nerves with the knowledge you have a professional looking out for your retirement money.

Of course your investment advocate can't guarantee he or she will be able to consistently achieve this goal, and it should only be used as a general guideline. Also, it will take time for you to fully appreciate and benefit from all the planning and monitoring provided by your advocate.

How Realistic Expectations Pay Off

I began working with several new clients in 2000, just as the stock market entered a horrendous three-year slide. It culminated in 2002, with the S&P 500 dropping a total of 44% over those three years. Prior to 2000, the S&P 500 had experienced an unprecedented 20%+ average annual return from 1995 through 1999.

Based on what they had experienced over the previous five years, my new clients' expectations were incredibly high. I had to work hard to convince them that while no one knew what the future held, the odds of 20%+ annual returns continuing was very low. I suggested they should expect a market "correction"—a Wall Street way of saying stocks will probably go down for a while—and invest accordingly.

Prudence dictated they should try to preserve and protect their retirement funds by lowering their lofty expectations and diversifying into fixed-income assets like bond funds and guaranteed investment contracts (GICs). Fortunately, they listened and agreed to diversify their stock-heavy portfolios based on my recommendations. None of them got rich during the three down years, but none lost much, and some came out ahead.

"Hire an Investment Advisor? Why? The Market's Doing Great!"

Of course, they had to endure the taunts and sneers of friends and associates who were managing their own retirement plans. These "experts" thought the big stock market gains would go on indefinitely. One client confided to me that his brother told him "bonds were for sissies" and that he was stupid to pay me a fee to do something he could do just as well himself.

Fortunately, because of his willingness to adopt prudent expectations and a disciplined investment process, my client rode out the 2000-2002 market crash relatively unscathed. Sadly, his brother wasn't as "lucky." Of course, past performance is no guarantee of future results and my future clients may not enjoy the same success as previous clients during a severe down market.

In working with your investment advocate, you should be able to develop reasonable expectations for the growth of your retirement assets over time. Having a well-thought-out, written plan that's monitored regularly should limit your temptation to stray from your long-term strategy when tempted by short-term investing fads.

Only Hogs Go Broke

In the stock market, investors who believe stocks are going up are called "bulls." Those who think its going down are called "bears." There's an old saying in the investment world that goes something like this: "Bulls make money and bears make money; only hogs go broke."

This means you can get reasonably good returns in a bull (up) market and you can get good returns in a bear (down) market. The investment strategy for each of these situations is based on a valid premise. But if you get hoggish, wanting more and bigger returns than anyone can reasonably expect, that's an invalid premise. By adopting it, you're setting yourself up for disappointment.

Yet reasonable expectations—though they're not exciting, and make for dull party talk—should go a long way toward helping you achieve long-term investment success.

Remember . . .

☞ As my friend Nido Qubein says, your basic premise is vital to your ultimate success.

☞ Even world-class money managers go through slumps, but they are usually only temporary. Smart managers don't suddenly become "stupid."

☞ While some of your money managers will occasionally under-perform, others will probably be doing exceptionally well. Focus on your total return.

☞ Reasonable expectations will help inoculate you from the deadly virus of constantly jumping from one "hot" investment to another.

☞ You and your advocate need to agree on what a reasonable return is at the beginning of your relationship. You can adjust it over time by amending your IPS.

Resource:

Learn how you could become a millionaire without really trying (too hard). Go to **retirerich-online.com** and click on the **"Rich"** link, then click on **"Easy Millionaire."**

SECRET #9

Milk Your Cash Cow of Moooooolah

*How to Turn Your Retirement Plan into
an Income-Generating Machine*

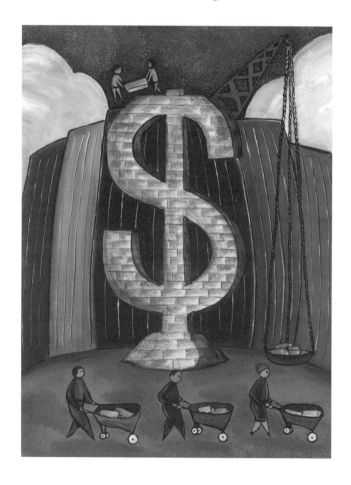

In this chapter you'll discover:

☞ Why investing for a steady stream of dependable retirement income is serious business.

☞ Why a well-diversified, income-generating portfolio should be less susceptible to wild market swings than a growth portfolio.

☞ Why you shouldn't take more than 6% of the portfolio value annually for income.

An investment that produces a steady stream of income is called a "cash cow." Like the daily milk that comes from a good Jersey or Holstein, this income pays the bills and keeps your "farm" running smoothly.

Investing your retirement funds for a steady, growing retirement income stream is serious business. Mess this up, and you'll have the rest of your life to regret it! So will your spouse, grandchildren and anyone else who may be depending on you financially.

It might seem like I'm exaggerating, but after watching nice, educated (but financially illiterate) people recklessly destroy their financial security, I'm quite passionate about this subject. Let me share a true story that illustrates the point.

In the late '90s I was teaching classes in retirement planning as an adjunct professor at James Madison University in Harrisonburg, Virginia. One of my students was a well-respected physician who'd recently retired after practicing medicine for 35 years.

"Dr. Jones" was sitting in on my class to see if he could pick up any helpful ideas. After the class he asked me to review his retirement portfolio and suggest any changes I thought might be appropriate. During our initial conversation, I learned he'd been managing his retirement plan investments himself and took some pride in how well he'd done to date.

Past Performance is Certainly NO Guarantee of Future Results!

It's important to remember that our visit occurred in the late 1990's, at the tail end of the longest-running bull market in the history of the United States. Unfortunately, Dr. Jones didn't realize that his positive investment results to date were due to a strong stock market, not his imagined investment skill.

Dr. Jones had accumulated nearly one million dollars, split almost evenly between his IRA and taxable brokerage account. He was taking out over $100,000 per year for income. This was about 12% of the value of his accounts. Since he was doing so well with his investments, he was also giving thousands of dollars away to his children every year.

He'd bought "mail-order" mutual funds from several different firms. And while he owned different funds, they were all invested in the same types of popular, hot growth stocks. I explained to Dr. Jones that he was dangerously over-concentrated in growth stocks, which made his retirement portfolio extremely vulnerable. (Remember what you read earlier about all your eggs in one basket? He was a textbook case.)

I went on to suggest that the stock markets were highly overvalued based on historical precedent and that he should immediately diversify his portfolio into income-oriented holdings to support the withdrawals he was taking to live on. I recommended an income-oriented portfolio that included:

- Balanced fund(s) (a combination of dividend-paying stocks and interest-paying bonds)
- Real estate fund
- International stock fund
- Equity income fund (comprised of stocks that pay high dividends)
- Corporate bond fund
- Government bond fund

In addition, I included a small portion allocated to funds of small- and middle-cap companies in order to give him growth potential over time. ("Cap" is short for "capitalization," which is defined as the number of shares outstanding times the dollar value of the shares. A company with one million shares outstanding, selling for $10 per share, has a "cap" of ten million dollars.)

Finally I suggested he should discontinue the gifting to his children and reduce his income withdrawals to no more than 6% of his total portfolio value in order to avoid eating into irreplaceable principal.

"Thanks, but no thanks, Sonny"

Dr. Jones gave me a grandfatherly smile and thanked me for my suggestions. Then in his deep doctor's voice, he told me how he'd been taking this income out of his accounts and making the gifts for the past three years, yet his accounts were still going up handsomely.

He reasoned that since the stock market had averaged about 11% growth annually for the past 75 years (according to Morningstar Mutual Funds), he could comfortably take that much out for income.

Besides, he said, he had a number of smart doctor friends whom he conferred with regularly, and they all were doing what he was doing, with outstanding results. How could that many doctors be wrong? To confirm this conviction, all his investment magazines and newsletters painted a rosy picture for stocks as far as the eye could see.

In a way, I pitied Dr. Jones because he was essentially gambling with his financial security. Once he blew his investments, he and his long-suffering wife would be reduced to getting by on their Social Security.

Three Years Later

I pretty much forgot about Dr. Jones, until he called about three years later. He wanted to meet with me to go over some old life insurance policies. When he came in, he had six or seven old whole-life policies, the kind that build cash value in addition to the death benefit.

He wanted to know how much cash he could take out of the policies. It turned out he had about $75,000 in cash values and the insurance company was only too happy to let him "borrow" this money at 6% interest.

It seemed the good doctor was experiencing a "temporary" cash flow crunch and he was desperately looking for some extra money to "tide him over." I didn't ask how his investments were doing (stocks had started their three-year slide two years earlier) and he didn't offer to tell me, so he just thanked me for my help and left.

"And now," as Paul Harvey says, "the rest of the story"

After he was gone, curiosity got the best of me and I pulled up his file on my computer. I still had his old portfolio saved and when I updated the values based on current market prices, minus the withdrawals he was making, my jaw literally dropped! The portfolio was worth about $400,000; less than half what it was worth three years earlier!

I can't say for sure if this was the case or not, because I don't know if he made any changes in his portfolio after our initial visit. I do know he probably wouldn't have been so keen to borrow cash from his life insurance polices if he wasn't hurting for money.

Then I updated the values in the recommended portfolio I'd suggested to him, which included diversifying for income and reducing his withdrawals to no more than 6% of the portfolio. The recommended portfolio was down too, but it was still worth over $900,000![1] Again, past performance is no guarantee of future results.

---

[1] According to Morningstar Advisor.com

Old Mr. Greed had gotten hold of Dr. Jones and caused him to ignore both common sense and sound advice. He'd made a natural mistake when he figured he could take large withdrawals every year from his investments without any problem.

You would think that if stocks have averaged around 11% growth over the long term you should be able to take that much out annually without touching your principal. But as he discovered, that is a very dangerous assumption.

The Key Secret to Investing for Retirement Income

Here's the little-known, but simple secret to turning your retirement plan into an income-producing cash cow that generates all the moooooolah you'll need to enjoy financial freedom!

Diversify your investments into income-producing assets and don't withdraw more than your account earns in dividends and interest.

At the very most, limit your withdrawals to no more than 6% of the account's value annually. The American Society of Certified Public Accountants suggests taking no more than 4 % to 5% , while the Financial Planning Association advises no more than 6%. Both organizations have done studies supporting these withdrawal rates as reasonable assumptions based on historical precedent. They know what they're talking about. And they don't try to practice medicine.

If keeping your withdrawals to these levels means adjusting your lifestyle, so be it. Better to live modestly within your means than stressfully outside them. If you've planned and calculated your needs properly, you should have enough money stashed away so you would never have to take more than the dividends and interest earned.

The Music Stops

Dr. Jones had been living on borrowed time because all the income he was withdrawing had come from gains in the value of his stock funds. He had the "bad" luck of retiring just as the stock market took off in early 1995 which created unreasonable expectations. When the bull market topped out in March of 2000, and stocks began their disastrous three-year slide, his portfolio literally fell off a cliff!

By diversifying your retirement plan into income-generating assets, you should be able to ride out the normal ups and downs of the market. The portfolio I'd recommended to Dr. Jones would have generated a steady cash flow from dividends and interest equal to about 6% of the account's value. So even when stocks began dropping, the income would have kept right on coming.

If you follow this Secret, you won't have to sell your stocks to come up with cash to live on when the market's declining. By the way, after three years of getting pounded, stocks rebounded in 2003 and 2004. By limiting the withdrawals to income only, the portfolio I recommended to Dr. Jones would have actually grown in value after five years!

Of course this is a hypothetical illustration and past performance is no guarantee of future results. But it sure does make you think!

There you have it: the secret to turning your retirement money into an income-producing cash cow so you can enjoy financial freedom without having to work. I want you to Retire Rich and Happy, with the mooooolah to live a long, prosperous, care-free life during your retirement years.

Remember . . .

☞ Investing for a steady stream of dependable retirement income is serious business. Don't play games with this or you'll have the rest of your life to regret it!

☞ A well-diversified, income-generating portfolio should be less susceptible to wild market swings than a growth portfolio.

☞ Don't take more than 6% of the portfolio value annually for income.

☞ To be even more conservative, limit your withdrawals to the actual income your portfolio is generating. This way you don't have to sell stocks in a declining market for cash flow.

☞ You can be a bull or a bear, but don't be a hog or you might get slaughtered like Dr. Jones!

Resource:

For more information on investing for income go to **retirerich-online.com** and click on the **"Rich"** link and then click on **"Milk Your Cash Cow."**

SECRET #10

"Buddy, Can You Spare a Dime?"

Protect Yourself When Sponsoring a Qualified Retirement Plan
—Or the Government Can Take EVERYTHING You Own

In this chapter you'll discover:

☞ Why you're subject to unlimited personal liability when you sponsor a retirement plan.

☞ How your investment advocate can help protect you.

☞ You are responsible for ensuring documentation of your responsibilities.

☞ Following the law isn't only smart, but should lead to superior investment results.

☞ How the right mutual funds can make a big difference in your ultimate results.

☞ Compliance doesn't have to be burdensome, time consuming or expensive.

In 1974, after 11 years of talking, arguing, posturing, politicking and compromising, Congress passed the Employee Retirement Income Security Act (ERISA). Retirement plan sponsors hate it. Government regulators love it. This law has many tough provisions, some of which were designed to put real teeth into the government's requirement that you, the business owner, protect your employees' money when you sponsor a qualified retirement plan.

In 1974, the vast majority of retirement plans were so-called Defined Benefit plans. These are the old type of pension plans which pay the participant a certain amount of money every month, depending upon length of service or other criteria. Because the benefit in such plans is defined, the business sponsoring the plan has to guarantee that the money will be there when the participant retires. This caused businesses with Defined Benefit plans to take great pains, hiring expensive consultants and actuaries to ensure the money would be prudently managed and indeed be available when the time came to start paying out the pensions.

A "Qualified" Retirement Plan generally allows you to deduct contributions to lower your income tax liability and allows the funds to grow tax free until withdrawal. Normally a 401(k), Pension or Profit Sharing plan.

Defined Benefit vs. Defined Contribution Plans

Nowadays, most Defined Benefit plans are offered only to government workers or to employees of large, well-established companies with huge, steady cash flows. Since such plans demand that the employer put in certain dollar amounts, they are much harder to keep funded. If the company has a bad year and cash flows are down, that's no excuse. The plan must be funded anyway.

Because of these difficulties, in the 1980s many companies, especially smaller ones, switched to 401(k) plans. These are Defined Contribution plans, which means the money for the pensions would all, or nearly all, come from the employees' paychecks, according to formulas set forth in the plan documents. Again, the contribution—the amount put in during working years—is defined, whereas in the older plans the benefit—the amount taken out at retirement—is defined.

New Law, New Rules

ERISA departed from previous laws in two important ways. First, the definition of a "fiduciary" was spelled out. A fiduciary is someone who holds a position of trust. If you set up a trust fund for the care of an elderly relative, the person who manages that fund is a fiduciary. If your lawyer collects money on your behalf and holds it for you, the lawyer is acting as a fiduciary.

Because fiduciaries are in positions where they must be trusted, the courts hold them to a very high standard of integrity, performance and accountability. Under ERISA, anyone who has control or influence over the money in a retirement plan is considered a fiduciary. That means you, as a business owner, are held to this high standard, and if you fail to meet it, you can get into trouble—a LOT of trouble. Read on.

The second change made by ERISA is the biggie. It says that, as a fiduciary, if you breach your duty, you are subject to unlimited personal liability! This means you, various corporate officers, your investment committee and the consultants you hire to help you manage the plan are required by law to follow a prudent process in managing a qualified retirement plan. If you don't, the government can take everything you own, and everything all those other people own too. Unlimited liability. And none of you can hide behind your corporation and say you're not liable. You are liable, personally. You could end up without a dime. Have I made this clear enough?

So what is a "prudent process"? If you have to ask, then you probably don't have one! The Foundation for Fiduciary Studies spells out a prudent process in *Prudent Investment Practices: A Handbook for Investment Fiduciaries.*

A fiduciary demonstrates prudence by the process through which investment decisions are managed, rather than by showing that investment products and techniques are chosen because they were labeled as "prudent." Most investments are not imprudent on their face. It is the way in which they are used, and how decisions as to their use are made that will be examined to determine whether the prudence standard has been met.

The book goes on to list the many practices which taken together constitute a prudent process. You, as a business owner, are responsible for ensuring this process is followed. By doing so, you'll dramatically reduce your exposure to unlimited personal liability. And, in the event of such a charge, you will have the documentation in hand to show that you are indeed following the required guidelines.

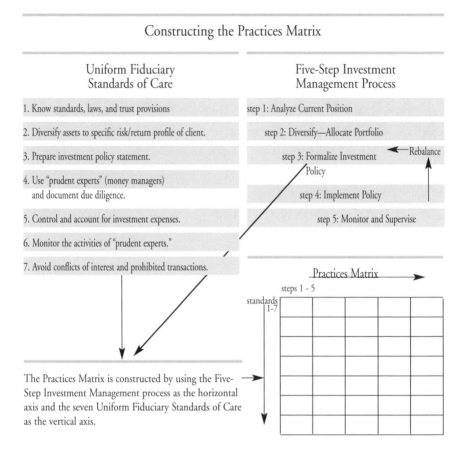

Constructing the Practices Matrix

Uniform Fiduciary Standards of Care	Five-Step Investment Management Process
1. Know standards, laws, and trust provisions	step 1: Analyze Current Position
2. Diversify assets to specific risk/return profile of client.	step 2: Diversify—Allocate Portfolio
3. Prepare investment policy statement.	step 3: Formalize Investment Policy
4. Use "prudent experts" (money managers) and document due diligence.	step 4: Implement Policy
5. Control and account for investment expenses.	step 5: Monitor and Supervise
6. Monitor the activities of "prudent experts."	
7. Avoid conflicts of interest and prohibited transactions.	

Rebalance

The Practices Matrix is constructed by using the Five-Step Investment Management process as the horizontal axis and the seven Uniform Fiduciary Standards of Care as the vertical axis.

Practices Matrix

steps 1 - 5

standards 1-7

The Practices

As the previous chart illustrates, the practices are made up of the Uniform Fiduciary Standards of Care, shown on the left, and the Five-Step Investment Management Process, shown on the right. By combining these standards and practices you'll ensure you're following a prudent process.

Now don't get angry at me for telling you about all this. I'm just pointing out what the law says. I'm not trying to scare you by pointing out the potential liability you face by sponsoring a qualified retirement plan. After all, the odds are good you'll never have an employee complaint or face a Department of Labor or IRS audit of your plan. But those things could happen.

Following the law is not only the right thing to do; it also increases your chances of enjoying reasonable investment results. Besides, whoever sold you your plan should be helping you meet this requirement now as part of their service. Unfortunately, from what I've seen, very few vendors do this, or at best they make a half-hearted attempt to do so. Yet compliance isn't that hard when you know how to do it, and it shouldn't cost you any more to implement.

Ignorance Is Not Bliss

Recently I reviewed the 401(k) plan for a medium-sized business to determine how well they were complying with their fiduciary duties under ERISA. Their plan provider, a large firm supposedly specializing in 401(k) plans, had indeed addressed the issues of fiduciary standards of care in a letter to the firm's Human Resources director.

In short, the letter said that the necessary steps were being taken to meet ERISA guidelines and everything was OK. As I read further, I noted the letter mentioned that rarely is it in the best interests of the plan to have all their mutual fund choices provided by a single fund family. It went on to say that doing so could mean the fiduciaries had failed to meet their obligations and therefore exposed themselves to unlimited personal liability.

You may be wondering why it's generally not a good idea to have all the mutual funds from a single company. Well even if a company has all kinds of different funds (Fidelity has over 100) they aren't all outstanding performers.

You have to document why the funds in your plan were a good choice for the employees. So you generally want to choose outstanding funds from various providers to show you were looking out for your employees.

Then I reviewed the 401(k) plan summary. On page 25, all the mutual fund investment choices were listed. I had to do a double-take because 16 of the 17 funds were all from the very same fund family! I couldn't believe it. Since one of the 17 funds was from a different family, the letter was technically correct—but just barely.

It would be up to the fiduciaries to provide documents supporting their decision to use one fund family for 94% of their mutual fund choices. Of course, no such documents existed. So in the event of a plan audit or employee complaint, the fiduciaries could find themselves in hot water. And one of the fiduciaries in that pot of boiling water was, of course, the owner of the business.

The Plot Thickens

As part of my analysis I compared the existing mutual fund choices to independent alternatives readily available in the market place. I went back five years to February 1, 2000 and assumed $60,000 had been invested in the eight primary asset classes, for a total of $480,000. Yes, I know I said there were 17 different funds, but some of them were almost carbon copies of each other. In reality, there were only eight different asset classes represented (see Secret #6 for more info).

Then I assumed $16,000 was added every year in equal amounts into the various funds on a quarterly basis—for a total investment of $560,000. The ending value as of January 31, 2005 was $718,791 for a gain of $158,791. This represented an annual return of 5.48% per year.[1] Not bad, considering how volatile stocks were during that period.

Next, I ran the numbers using the independent mutual funds, assuming the same amount of money was invested at precisely the same time. The results were interesting. The alternative funds would have generated a gain of $304,249 with an ending value of $864,249. This represented an annual return of 9.68% per year—almost twice as much as the existing funds, which were all from the same fund family!

---

[1] Source: Morningstar Advisor.com

Amazingly, the alternative funds I used weren't the best performing funds in their asset classes. They were just funds I was familiar with, having used them regularly with existing clients. Now, of course past performance is no guarantee of future results, but it sure does open your eyes.

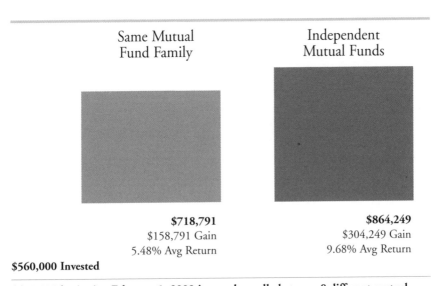

Same Mutual Fund Family	Independent Mutual Funds
$718,791	**$864,249**
$158,791 Gain	$304,249 Gain
5.48% Avg Return	9.68% Avg Return

$560,000 Invested

$480,000 beginning February 1, 2000 invested equally between 8 different mutual funds with $4,000 added quarterly through January 31, 2005. $560,000 total invested.

Complying with ERISA

As I mentioned earlier, compliance isn't that tough when you know what to do. Your investment advocate should have this down pat and be able to provide the documentation necessary to ensure you're meeting your obligations. He or she should provide you with regular fund progress reports and show you how well your money managers are doing compared to their peers.

In addition, you should receive quarterly or semi-annual reports on the entire portfolio. This will show the breakdown of stocks invested in large, medium and small companies; foreign stocks; bonds—their quality and duration; cash; expenses; total returns and more. This doesn't have to be complicated. Your investment advocate can provide this information on a single page.

After you and the investment committee review the portfolio summary, a copy goes into your file, along with the minutes from the meeting. Ta-da! You're well on your way to meeting your fiduciary requirements. Remember, it's the process that's important. So by documenting the fact that you are following a prudent process as outlined in the practices, you should be OK.

You'll sleep better knowing that you're following the law and you're also keeping track of what's going on with your retirement money. Plus, in the rare event that an audit or complaint does crop up, you can whip out the documents prepared by your investment advocate. Unlimited personal liability is scary, but by following these proven steps you'll protect yourself from having to take a post on street corners, begging for dimes!

Remember . . .

☞ As a business owner, you're subject to unlimited personal liability when you sponsor a qualified retirement plan.

☞ Your investment advocate can help protect you by providing the necessary reports to prove you're in compliance. You are responsible for ensuring this is being done correctly.

☞ Following the law isn't only smart, but should lead to superior investment results.

☞ The right mutual funds can make a big difference in your ultimate results.

☞ Compliance doesn't have to be burdensome, time consuming or expensive.

Additional resources:

■ Fiduciary 360 is the premier resource to help plan fiduciaries understand their responsibilities and learn how to ensure they are compliant. **http://www.fi360.com**

■ Reish, Luftman, Reicher & Cohen is one of the top law firms dedicated to assisting business owners with ERISA issues. **http://www.reish.com**

■ U. S. Department of Labor ERISA information **http://www.dol.gov/dol/compliance/comp-erisa.htm**

■ Internal Revenue Service ERISA information **http://www.irs.gov/retirement/article/0,,id=103022,00.html**

SECRET #11

"Thank God for _____"
(your name here)

*Change the World; How Your Retirement Plan Can
Leave a Positive Legacy* Forever

In this chapter you'll discover:

☞ Why leaving your retirement plan to your heirs could be a tax disaster.

☞ By leaving your plan assets to a private family foundation or a donor-advised fund, you can create valuable benefits for your heirs and for society, while avoiding paying taxes.

☞ By choosing such an alternative, you help your family learn and grow together, while putting your money to work, doing good forever!

☞ Lump-sum charitable bequests are irrevocable. You should only leave lump sums to organizations with years of proven stability and good stewardship.

You've lived a long, fulfilling life and now it's time to meet your maker. The money in your retirement plan has grown over the years because you hired a wonderful investment advocate who's taken good care of you. Your advocate helped you begin with the end in mind by asking you thoughtful questions about what your ideal life and retirement lifestyle would look like, and then putting your answers down on paper so you could focus on them regularly.

You have a well-drafted Investment Policy Statement, which included the rationale for your diversified income and growth portfolio. From time to time, your advocate suggested adjustments to your IPS based on your changing needs, market conditions and manager performance. You felt comfortable over the years, secure in the knowledge that your advocate's interests were aligned with yours since they were paid a fee for good advice, not commissions for transactions.

When you retired, you limited your withdrawals to no more than the dividends and interest earned. This helped you ride out stock market volatility over the years relatively unscathed.

Your Retirement Plan Could Be a Tax Bomb

Your advocate pointed out that the tax laws create liabilities for your heirs if you leave your retirement plan to them when you die. Since the money in the plan has been accumulating over the years tax-deferred, then whoever inherits your plan would owe taxes at the highest tax rates.

Plus, all the money in the plan would be included in the value of your estate, possibly adding more tax liability. Your advocate told you there had been some cases where up to 75% of the value of a business owner's retirement plan had been taxed away when he died!

Make a Better Choice

Your advocate suggested you may want to consider another alternative. Instead of leaving your retirement plan to your children or grandchildren, why not:

- leave a lasting legacy for good by supporting worthy charities forever;

- use it to teach your family about the value of charitable giving;

- use it to keep your family in touch over the years;

- use it to teach your family universal laws that will benefit them for generations;

- give the money that would have gone to taxes to the charities of your choice.

Your advocate pointed out that you have plenty of other assets, especially after selling the business. You've already taken steps to ensure your family will be cared for after you're gone without them becoming trust-baby brats! And you've already been making generous charitable gifts because you understand the importance of giving back to your community.

Depending on the value of your retirement plan, you could leave it to:

- A private family foundation
- A donor-advised fund

In order to maintain family harmony, I suggest a corporate trustee should be used to manage bequests from this fund based on your instructions. Of course you could leave it up to your kids to decide who to give the money to, but that could create unwanted conflict—and you don't want hard feelings to be your legacy.

You would need to speak with your attorney to determine which entity made the most sense for you. This approach enables your family to learn about the various charities you support and why you support them. It avoids all the taxes (income and estate), since these entities qualify as charitable organizations.

Every winter the corporate trustee would hold a family meeting at a nice sunny resort (paid for by your legacy trust) to report on the fund's progress and to explain which charities received money and what they're doing with it. You could even stipulate that a certain amount of financial education be part of the family meeting to help your family learn how to be good stewards.

Your grandchildren and great grandchildren will learn about the joy of giving without expecting anything in return. And they will learn why they need to make charitable giving, of their own resources, a priority in their lives.

Warning: Lump-Sum Charitable Gifts Are Irrevocable!

Of course, you could just leave your entire estate to a charity when you die and be done with it. That's the easy way, but it may not be the best way to give. There's nothing wrong with leaving a lump-sum gift to a well-managed charity with a proven track record of good stewardship. And by all means, ask to see the charity's Investment Policy Statement and confirm that it's being followed before considering any type of lump-sum gift.

But what happens if the charity changes direction, after you've made the gift? What if you're conservative and after you're gone a bunch of godless radicals manage to worm their way into control of the charity and begin supporting causes you detest? Don't say it can't happen because it has. If you make a lump-sum gift at your death, that's it. Because it can't be revoked, your family can never get the money back!

If you've been supporting various charities faithfully over the years, by setting up a family foundation or donor-advised fund with the rest of your retirement funds, you can continue to support them after you're gone—in an even more direct way.

Plus, by having your corporate trustee decide whom to send checks to, you protect your loved ones from needless squabbles. The annual family retreat could be paid for by the money you leave in your trust and it could include much more than making decisions about charitable gifts.

Let's Do It!

The more you think about this idea, the more sense it makes. Your attorney suggests you name a donor-advised fund as the beneficiary to your retirement plan. He says the family foundation works best if you have ten million dollars or more to contribute because of the legal and accounting fees.

The donor-advised fund is much simpler to implement and maintain. Plus it provides practically all the tax-saving benefits of the family foundation.

The paperwork's all done and you feel much better knowing you won't be leaving a potential tax liability for your loved ones to deal with. The charitable organizations that are important to you will continue to receive support, provided they maintain the standards you dictate.

Plus, you'll be helping your family by including them in the process and teaching them profitable life lessons, like the value of giving.

Your retirement plan doesn't have to die with you. It can live on perpetually, sowing blessings into the lives of your family and those less fortunate. The lives you touch this way will never be the same. So thank God for _____ (insert your name) because you've left an enduring legacy that can change the world for good—forever!

Remember...

☞ If you leave your retirement plan to your heirs, the tax liability could eat up most of it.

☞ By leaving your plan assets to a private family foundation or a donor-advised fund, you can create valuable benefits for your heirs and for society, while avoiding paying taxes.

☞ By choosing such an alternative, you help your family learn and grow together, while putting your money to work, doing good forever!

☞ Lump-sum charitable bequests are irrevocable. You should only leave lump sums to organizations with years of proven stability and good stewardship. Ask to see the charity's Investment Policy Statement and confirm that it's being followed before considering a gift.

Resource:

Learn how you could use a charitable tax-advantaged trust to sell stocks, real estate or even a business without paying any capital gains tax. Go to **retirerich-online.com** and click on the **"Rich"** link, then click on **Tax Advantaged Trusts.**

SECRET #12

How to Retire Rich and Happy
Three Steps to a Balanced Life

In this chapter you'll discover:

☞ Why money is not the root of all evil.

☞ Being rich doesn't guarantee happiness.

☞ The Three Steps to a Balanced Life.

☞ You have to DO IT!

☞ You deserve to Retire Rich and Happy.

In Secret #1, I wrote about the value of making time for the really important things in life, like relationships, family and spiritual health. Having money is nice, but if your sole focus is on accumulating more and more wealth, I can promise you that you won't be very happy.

Money is nothing but a tool; it's neither good nor bad. It's gotten a bad rap because of a common misquotation from the Bible which says, "Money is the root of all evil." Actually, it doesn't say that at all. It says: *"For the **love** of money is a root of all kinds of evil..."* (1st Timothy 6:10 New King James Version). Some biblical scholars point out that the word which was translated as "money" originally meant "hoarded wealth," that is, money kept out of circulation.

We get to choose how we use our money and those choices will have a great impact on the quality of the lives we live. If you're still working on accumulating wealth, you're probably thinking, "If I were rich, I know I'd be happy too!"

But life doesn't work like that. Stop for a minute and think of all the rich and famous people from recent history who obviously weren't very happy.

■ Ernest Hemingway, world-renowned, successful writer (suicide)

■ Elvis Presley, entertainer (drug overdose)

■ Marilyn Monroe, movie star (drug overdose)

■ John Belushi, comic, movie star (drug overdose)

■ O. J. Simpson, football star (unhappy marriage, probably murdered his wife)

■ Bernie Ebbers, ex-corporate CEO (convicted felon)

Of course, these people were all well-known and in the public eye. Maybe regular folks without the pressure of being a recognized star would do better. Let's consider all those regular folks who strike it rich in the lottery. An awful lot of people play the lottery and they're convinced that when they hit it big, they'll be financially secure and happy for the rest of their lives.

Sadly, the facts suggest otherwise. Consider this article from the *Detroit Free Press* (July 21, 2004):

Lottery Winners Can Become Losers

Ever wonder what happens to folks who win the lottery? Or even more significantly, what happens to their money? A little digging into the lives of several winners turns up some surprising and disturbing answers. And it's clear hitting the lottery jackpot does not necessarily lead to happily ever after.

It was just 11 years ago that Suzanne Mullins won more than $4 million in the Virginia lottery. Today, she not only is broke, she's $154,000 in debt.

Hard to believe? Not for Tom Nasta. He's a personal financial planner in Roanoke. Tom says it's not unusual for people to go broke after winning the lottery. He had a client who won $1 million and within seven years, all he had left to show for it was a mobile home.

I could go on, but you get the picture. Money, fame and popularity don't guarantee a happy, fulfilling life. Rich people have the same day-to-day problems as everyone else. But some of them have discovered they can be Rich <u>and</u> Happy. How do they do it? In a word, balance.

Three Steps to a Balanced Life

My own epiphany occurred after the deaths of my brother and father. Fortunately I learned about the importance of balance before I lost my marriage, relationships with my children and spiritual compass. Interestingly, I discovered that my business became *more profitable* after I determined to lead a balanced life.

Step One is the most important. It's when you make the conscious decision that there must be a better way to live, and you are going to find it, no matter what. Don't worry if you're feeling frustrated. That's good! Frustrated people are willing to do what's necessary to change.

Step Two is when you commit your new lifestyle to writing. I call it your Lifestyle Blueprint™. This takes time and effort, but the rewards are infinitely worth it. You may need help with this step. Go to my website at **www.retirerich-online.com** and click on **"Happy"** then click on the **Lifestyle Blueprint™** for more info.

Step Three requires you to make a commitment to stay focused on your balanced life. You'll need to check yourself regularly to make sure you stay on course, just like sea captains used their sextants to navigate by the stars. I can promise you that you'll be tempted to fall back into your old lifestyle habits, but if you do, what do you suppose will happen?

The best way to stay focused is to have accountability. You need someone (life coach, spouse, advocate) who understands your commitment and will work with you on an on-going basis to keep you on track. Your spouse will be the first to notice if you're veering off the path, so listen carefully to his or her feedback.

The Results?

In Secret #1, I described how I ultimately decided to make some drastic changes in my life because I'd become so overly focused on business success. You may be wondering how things have worked out and if my "conversion" was real.

Thankfully, the answer is a resounding Yes! It took a while for me to adjust to my new schedule. I'd become addicted to stress and needed pressure to feel like I was accomplishing my goals. When I made the decision to change to a more balanced life, I felt guilty at first when I took time off.

For instance, I decided to make Wednesday my day to recharge my batteries. I could do anything I wanted, and often that meant flying my airplane. It felt kind of strange to be piloting an Angel Flight mission on a sunny Wednesday morning instead of slaving away at my desk.

I discovered the gratitude expressed by the families I was helping gave me a sense of accomplishment and renewed energy I hadn't known before. I believe this time off has helped me serve my clients better because I'm not as subject to burn-out.

Don't Be Afraid to Wave Your Magic Wand

As DeAnn and I spent more time together, we would talk about our ideal life and what it would look like if we could wave that magic wand. Because her father was in the Air Force, she lived in the Philippines as a little girl. Ever since, she has loved warm weather and was finding the cold, dark winters in the Shenandoah Valley difficult to take.

I love the water and held a vivid memory of a dream vacation on a lake in North Carolina with my family when I was 12 years old. I spent many hours happily snorkeling along the shore and reveled in the natural beauty of the lake. What if we could live somewhere a little warmer and on a lake?

Why not?

Our girls were all grown up and essentially independent. The business was doing well and I could continue serving my clients anywhere in the country with an Internet connection and cell phone. Plus, my assistant, Jean, was experienced and capable of handling routine client service requests on a daily basis.

A few months later we were planning a trip to Florida to attend an air show. As I studied the flight maps, I noticed the lakes around Charlotte, North Carolina and made a mental note to follow up. On our return flight home to Virginia we landed in Rock Hill, South Carolina, just below Charlotte, to refuel. We discovered Lake Wylie, which was built by Duke Power in 1903 to generate hydroelectricity. It was close to the airport and it was gorgeous!

Once we were back home I began researching the Lake Wylie area on the Internet and liked what I saw. It was close to a dynamic, growing major city (Charlotte, NC) with all the cultural opportunities this provides. The climate was temperate, with mild winters and summers and there were new homes for sale on the lake.

DeAnn and I flew down a few weeks later and started looking at houses with our new friend and realtor, Don Westmoreland. Don was very easy to work with. He's calm, laid back and very knowledgeable about the area, having grown up nearby. And since his father is a contractor, he knows quality houses and who the good home-builders are. With his help, we located a new home on the lake and bought it.

Things started coming together almost magically! We sold our house in Virginia and within two months we were moving into our new home on the lake. Best of all, the Rock Hill airport was only 10 minutes away, so I would be close to my airplane. The airport even had a hangar available so my "baby" didn't have to stay outside.

Just Do It!

It's nice to talk about changing. Thinking about it is nice too. But ultimately, you have to put thoughts into action and do whatever it takes to live the rich, fulfilling life you were created for. I hope this book has sparked you into thinking about the possibility of living the life you've always dreamed of. And has helped you understand the "secrets" to managing the finances you'll need to live that life. Yes, there are people who Retire Rich and Happy—but it didn't just happen to them because they were lucky.

Either consciously or unconsciously, they made a decision to live their lives in such a way that they had time for the really important things. They chose to do what they had to in order to accumulate enough money to afford the lives they wanted.

They chose to make time for their spouses, families and friends. They recognized the value of spiritual growth and the joy of giving back to their community. They're not perfect people and their lives are far from perfect.

But they did Retire Rich and Happy, and you deserve to be one of them too!

Remember...

☞ Money is neither good nor bad; it's simply a tool.

☞ The love of money (not money itself) is the root of all evil.

☞ Being rich doesn't guarantee happiness.

☞ Follow the Three Steps to a Balanced Life.

☞ You have to DO IT!

☞ You deserve to Retire Rich and Happy.

Resource:

Go to my website **retirerich-online.com**, and click on the **"Happy"** link for more information on living the life you've always dreamed of.

BONUS SECRET

No Retirement Plan? No Problem!

Here are two tax-advantaged strategies you can use to build your retirement nest-egg without having to include your employees or deal with government red tape.

This Secret will be helpful to you if you fall into one of the following categories:

☞ You have a qualified retirement plan, but want to put more money aside than you can now because of government restrictions.

☞ You don't have a retirement plan, but want to put money aside in a tax-advantaged way.

☞ You don't want to deal with the red tape, hassle and unlimited personal liability that come with tax-qualified retirement plans.

☞ You don't want to put money in for employees because you already pay them well.

The idea of putting money aside for retirement makes good sense, but some business owners need more choices than the government's rules allow. If you find yourself in any of the above categories, cheer up. I have good news for you! Here are two tax-smart strategies that may enable you to accumulate substantial funds for retirement so you can enjoy the financial freedom to do what you want, when you want.

Unlike traditional retirement plans that dictate how much you can contribute, both of these strategies are exempt from any dollar limit whatsoever. So you can put in as much as you like, as often as you like. Granted, the tax advantages may not be as substantial as those generated by a traditional retirement plan. But there are advantages nonetheless, so let's look at them.

Take hypothetical clients Bill and Sally. Bill is 53 years old and runs a successful cement business. He contributes to a Simple IRA. He also matches a portion of his employees' contributions. The problem is, Bill is earning over $400,000 per year but can only contribute about $14,000 annually to his retirement plan.

He and Sally, age 50, want to put more money away. They've always lived within their means and feel they can comfortably save an extra $100,000 per year to supplement their retirement. They're looking forward to retiring in about 10 years. Bill's investment advocate suggests that a tax-sensitive portfolio may be what he and Sally need in order to accumulate the additional retirement nest-egg they desire.

What's a "Tax-Sensitive" Portfolio?

By using certain types of investments, you can put together a portfolio that has a major objective of avoiding or putting off paying taxes—both of which are legal. Mind you, the main objective is still to make money—in the form of dividends, interest and capital growth. The investments are selected for their ability to make money, but in ways that receive favorable tax treatment.

Tax-Sensitive Portfolio

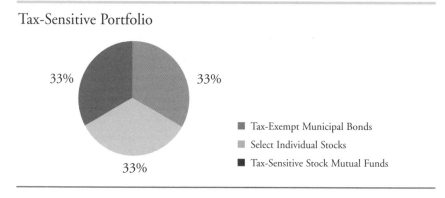

33%   33%

■ Tax-Exempt Municipal Bonds
■ Select Individual Stocks
33%   ■ Tax-Sensitive Stock Mutual Funds

Here's how it would be set up. A fee-based brokerage account is established for Bill and Sally and is invested in the following manner:

Let's say Bill and Sally started their plan with a $100,000 contribution in January of 2000, just as the stock market was tanking. With all the bad market news, Mr. Fear would have a chance to work overtime on their emotions. But their investment advocate had created a reasonable Investment Policy Statement, and often reminded them of the value of making regular investments.

Now what if they had invested in the S&P 500 index instead of the tax- sensitive portfolio? Well $100,000 invested every January 1 beginning in 2000 would have grown to $533,507 by December 31, 2004. That's an average annual return of 2.17% net after taxes.

However, if they invested the same money at the same time, but used our tax-sensitive portfolio, they would have wound up with $806,299 on December 31, 2004. Big difference! That's an average annual return of a little over 9% net after taxes and fees. Of course, this is a hypothetical example and past performance is no guarantee of future results.[1]

Now, if Bill and Sally just keep this up for the full ten years and manage to average the same 9% net, they would have approximately $1,650,000 to supplement their retirement. And if they began taking 6% of the account value annually, this would generate almost $100,000 per year in income for the rest of their lives!

Remember, this is a very simple strategy that:

- avoids government red tape;
- avoids unlimited personal liability;
- avoids additional accounting and auditing;
- avoids limits on what you can contribute and when you can take it out;
- avoids you having to put one penny into anybody's retirement account but your own.

Yes, you do give up the ability to deduct the contributions on your tax return. That is, you're using after-tax dollars rather than pre-tax dollars in a qualified plan. But if you use a tax-sensitive portfolio, you really don't give up much once the money is invested and you continue to enjoy the freedom to do what you want with your money, when you want.

[1] Source: Morningstar Advisor.com

So You Want Tax Deductions Too?

If Bill and Sally wanted more tax savings, such as being able to use pre-tax dollars to fund their retirement, they could consider another option. It has some wonderful features, including:

- They can contribute as much money as they want whenever they want.

- The money can be invested in stocks, bonds, mutual funds.

- The account grows tax-deferred, just like a traditional retirement plan.

- They receive a tax deduction whenever they make a contribution.

- Unlike a traditional retirement plan, the money they contribute is no longer included in the value of their estate for estate tax purposes.

- The money is exempt from the claims of creditors if they are ever sued.

- They can begin taking withdrawals whenever they want without penalties.

Let's assume they earn 9% net on the invested assets and, as in the tax-sensitive portfolio above, they invest $100,000 every year for 10 years ($1 million). However, they place their investments inside a tax-advantaged retirement trust, so they enjoy tax deductions with every contribution. In fact, based on current calculations, if they contributed the full million, they would have generated almost $200,000 ($193,790 to be exact) in charitable tax deductions![1]

While the tax deductions are nice, Bill and Sally would have given up their freedom to use the money for any purpose they chose. They can't touch the money in this trust until they're ready to retire. But once they do, they can take an income of about $100,000 per year to supplement their retirement. This money is paid to them as long as they live. And if the account grew, their income would grow along with it. However, once they both passed away, the money in the trust

---

[1] Source: Crescendo

would transfer to a donor-advised fund for charitable distributions; it wouldn't go to their family.

Of course Bill and Sally probably have other assets they could give the kids. There is no law that says you have to leave all your money to your children and grandchildren. So, if Bill and Sally really want the tax savings, and they are charitably inclined, this strategy may make sense for them. Or for you.

Summary

If you don't have a qualified retirement plan, or if you want to put more money aside than your plan allows, don't despair. Using these strategies, you'll be able to accumulate additional funds for retirement and enjoy some tax advantages. Best of all, you can put as much aside as you like without Uncle Sam getting in the way.

Remember . . .

☞ Because of government restrictions, qualified retirement plans may not allow you to invest enough money to fund a comfortable retirement.

☞ You can invest for retirement on a tax-advantaged basis without having a qualified retirement plan in place.

☞ A tax-sensitive portfolio limits your exposure to tax liability and gives you complete freedom from government regulations.

☞ You can enjoy attractive tax deductions and tax-deferral by using a tax-advantaged retirement trust.

☞ The tax-advantaged retirement trust enjoys attractive benefits, but there are trade-offs too.

Appendix A

Angel Flight Article Reprint

Angel Flight

Harrisonburg pilot Jeff Harris gives ill people a lift—literally

Daily News Record

Friday April 18, 2003

Story by: Brad Jenkins

Photos by: Mike Reilly

Somewhere above New York, where mountains look like mere hills and roads like skinny, squiggly snakes, Kimberly LaHart is asleep, oblivious to the scenery below.

LaHart has been asleep since the plane took off in Pittsburgh, Pa., about an hour ago. Nothing—not a fast takeoff or a choppy approach to the airport at her destination—has jolted her from the slumber.

Jeff Harris, meanwhile, is in the pilot's seat, listening to flight control on his headset, watching his plane inch along the map on a global-positioning system and occasionally adjusting levers as he cruises at 200 mph about 8,000 feet above the ground.

Harris, of Harrisonburg, is a volunteer with Angel Flight, a group

that provides free flights for ill patients. He is one of about 30 pilots in western Virginia who offer the service.

Not until the three tires of Harris' Cirrus airplane rumble

onto runway six in Elmira, N.Y., does LaHart fully wake up.

Here, she'll transfer to another plane flown by another Angel Flight pilot for a quick jaunt to Queensbury, N.Y., where she lives.

In all, it's about a three-hour trip from Pittsburgh to her home when LaHart flies.

Riding in a car would have meant eight uncomfortable hours for LaHart, who is still weak and tired three years after having multiple organ transplants.

LaHart's most recent trip to Pittsburgh—her 10th on an Angel Flight—was part of a routine check-up following a liver, pancreas, bowel and bone marrow transplant three years ago.

In her frail condition, LaHart has temporarily given up driving, and finding someone to drive her is difficult since her friends have to work.

Steve Patterson, executive vice president of Angel Flight Mid-Atlantic, says LaHart's situation is common. "Many of the patients we serve don't even have a car that could make it" to the hospital, he says.

Angel Flight flew 10,000 missions last year, serving about 2,600 people, Patterson says.

Angel Flight uses nearly 5,000 volunteer pilots like Harris who donate their time and planes with no reimbursement.

The corporate office sends out e-mail alerts when a patient needs a flight. Interested pilots then send a note back, and Angel Flight coordinates the mission, which could require connecting or non-stop planes.

Curt Hartman of Harrisonburg started flying missions three years ago after a friend died of cancer. He and that friend had enjoyed flying together.

At about the same time, an Angel Flight mission crashed near New Market, and the two events sparked something in Hartman.

"It's a real good example of what people can do with light aircraft. You can really do some good for a community," says Hartman, who flies a Piper Navajo.

Not just any pilot can fly for Angel Flight. A volunteer must be able to navigate using instruments and must have 250 hours of in-command flight time.

Hartman's job at Hartman Motor Sales in Harrisonburg is somewhat flexible, so he can fit the missions in as he has time.

Harris' flexible job as a financial planner has allowed him to donate his time, too.

At his day job at Jeff Harris & Associates Inc., Harris assists wealthy clients manage their wealth. When he takes an Angel Flight, he sometimes sees people at their lowest.

"I've been amazingly blessed with a good marriage and healthy children," Harris says. "These people have serious health problems. If I can do something to make that a little better, then I feel a sense of satisfaction."

It's a satisfaction rooted in snippets of memories about patients he has flown to areas as far as Indianapolis.

Patients like Andrea Mangum, who is married with three children.

When Harris picked Mangum up in Pittsburgh during his first year as an Angel Flight pilot last year, she didn't say much. The prognosis for the cancer growing inside her wasn't good.

"I saw her when she was probably at her lowest," Harris said.

But in a letter he later received, the woman wrote that the tumor was gone. Harris, who sometimes prays with the people he flies, calls it a "miraculous event."

Mangum's letter is now displayed on a poster with photos of his Angel Flight missions.

Hartman's patients have left impressions on him, too. A newborn who had to have heart surgery. A young kid with cancer whose happy, talkative nature reminded Hartman of his own son.

The pilots have left impressions on the patients, too.

One woman who flew with Harris was stunned when she saw Harris' plane, which he had just bought at the time.

"You mean you'd fly someone like me in your new plane?" the woman asked.

"That impacts them—that someone cares enough to do something for them," Harris says.

Appendix B

Saving 401(k)s from Disaster

Saving 401(k)s from Disaster:

Professionally Managed Accounts Grow in Popularity
by Jeff Harris, ChFC

On December 1, 2004 a headline on page one of *The Wall Street Journal* disclosed a huge and growing problem. It said in part, "…Many Mismanage Their 401(k)s." The subhead continued: "Workers Often Make Bad Picks In Saving for Retirement; Now, Some Let a Pro Do It."

What does this mean? And more importantly, why should you care?

The term "401(k)" refers to the Internal Revenue Code section that enables businesses to set up tax-deferred retirement plans. When first allowed by Congress in 1981, the plans were designed for "do-it-yourself" investors—people with small amounts to invest who were expected to manage the money themselves, rather than hiring professional managers.

American businesses responded enthusiastically, to the point where now approximately 42 million employees are in such plans. According to Watson Wyatt Worldwide, employee benefit consultants, these plans contain an estimated $1.9 trillion in assets. That's almost two thousand *billion* dollars!

One reason 401(k)s became so popular was that the stock market enjoyed unusually high returns during the 1980s and '90s. According to Towers Data, the S&P 500 with dividends reinvested increased an average of 17.84% per year during those two decades.

Even people who had no clue how to invest just about couldn't go wrong, since nearly everything was going up. Many novice 401(k) investors became convinced stocks would continue surging indefinitely. As the new millennium dawned, this naïve assumption would cost many participants dearly.

Unfortunately, the old 401(k) rules had a fatal flaw. They would not allow sponsoring companies to offer employees investment advice. They could provide educational seminars, fancy web sites, four-color newsletters and examples of portfolios. But in the end the choices were left up to the participants. In a rising market, this was not a problem. In a weak market, it held the seeds of disaster.

The Stock Bubble Bursts—and Congress Acts

In March of 2000 the stock market turned south, but many 401(k) investors thought the party was still going strong. Who could blame them? The financial press was suggesting new technology had made the business cycle of market ups and downs obsolete, and stocks would keep going up, seemingly forever! Investors wanted to believe this fairy tale, so they held on, hoping for more big returns in the coming years.

Alas, it was not to be. From 2000 to 2002 the S&P 500 dropped over 44%. The NASDAQ, home of the darling technology stocks, was down 86%.

Many 401(k) investors saw their portfolios drop dramatically, wiping out years of gains. At the time, Alicia Munnell, director of Boston College's Center for Retirement Research, said the do-it-yourself aspects of 401(k) plans "are not working."

Recognizing this, Congress changed the 401(k) rules in December 2001, enabling participants to hire professional fee-based advisors to help them manage and monitor their retirement plans.

Though the market today has recovered much of the losses of the past four years, the future is still uncertain. The Federal Reserve is raising interest rates. The prices of stocks relative to their earnings (the P/E ratios) are still fairly high.

Add in the danger of more terrorist attacks, high energy prices and the Iraq War, and you have a very challenging scenario for investors, especially 401(k) participants trying to manage their funds by themselves.

A Tale of Three Investors

Let's look at three hypothetical 401(k) investors and go back to November 1, 1999. They're all age 50, have $500,000 in their accounts, and are adding $10,000 every year.

Investor #1 has been reading financial magazines and is convinced technology is the place to put his money. So he invests everything in the NASDAQ stock index, loaded with technology and other small start-up companies. Two months after he made this move he's up over 30% and he's thrilled! At this rate he figures he can retire late next year.

Investor #2 also reads financial magazines and watches nightly business reports. He's more conservative and figures if he stays with the "big companies" he'll be OK. So he puts everything in the S&P 500 stock index, which is comprised of the 500 biggest companies in America. By the end of two months he's up almost 10%. He figures he can retire in three years.

Investor #3 hires an advisor who develops a disciplined investment strategy for him using asset allocation (a fancy term for not putting all your eggs in one basket). He divides his money among stock funds of large, medium and small companies, adding in some foreign funds and real estate funds. He tops it all off with some government bond funds for stability.

The advisor explains that every quarter the portfolio will be re-balanced to take advantage of normal market fluctuations. The advisor charges an annual fee of 1/2 of 1% of the portfolio's value.

After two months, Investor #3 is up a little over 5%. After hearing his buddies bragging in the break room about how well they're doing, he's wondering if he'd made the right decision.

Fast-forward five years. On October 31, 2004, here's how they did, according to Morningstar Mutual Funds. Remember they all started out with $500,000 and added $10,000 per year.

	Ending Value	Percent Gain(Loss)	Gain(Loss)
Investor #1	$382,401	(36.8%)	($167,599)
Investor #2	$502,648	(9.35%)	($47,352)
Investor #3	$774,472	36.95*	+$224,472*

* after deduction of all fees and expenses

Mind you, this is completely hypothetical. Past performance is no guarantee of future results and hiring a professional investment advisor may not improve performance.

But back in late 1999 with the stock market soaring and the popular financial press cheering it on, only a minority of 401(k) participants had the discipline to buck the trend and stick with an appropriately diversified portfolio.

A Trend Toward Sense and Stability

The message is clear: Congress wants 401(k) participants to have the option of using professional investment advisors if they don't want to "go it alone."

When the law was changed, it began a trend that you will see growing as forward-thinking, employee-focused companies begin offering their 401(k) participants the opportunity to hire professional investment help.

And that's good, because with a safe and comfortable retirement on the line, the stakes are too high to leave important investment decisions to amateurs.

Jeff Harris, Chartered Financial Consultant (ChFC), is a registered principal with Raymond James Financial Services, Inc. and manages the branch at 410 Neff Ave in Harrisonburg, VA. He is the past president of the Blue Ridge Chapter of the Virginia Society of CPAs and is a graduate of the Cannon School of Wealth Management at Northwestern University. Mr. Harris is an instrument-rated private pilot and is a volunteer pilot for Angel Flight. He can be reached with questions or comments at 800-296-2680 and his web site is www.raymondjames.com/jharris.

Appendix C

Investment Policy Statement (IPS) — Individual Investors

RAYMOND JAMES
ASSET MANAGEMENT SERVICES

INVESTMENT POLICY STATEMENT

Walter and Janet White

Approved on (date): _____

Presented by:

Jeffrey Harris
410 Neff Ave., Suite 200
Harrisonburg, VA 22801

This investment policy statement should be reviewed and updated at least annually. Any change to this policy should be communicated in writing on a timely basis to all interested parties.

Portfolio Summary:

Type of Plan:	Taxable
Current Assets:	$1,297,000
Time Horizon:	Short (3-5 years)
	Primary stage: 1 to 5 years
	Secondary stage: 1 to 5 years

Table of Contents

Part I - Purpose

The purpose of this Investment Policy Statement (IPS) is to provide written and formal financial goals and objectives.

Part II - Roles and Responsibilities

This section defines who is responsible and for what function.

Part III - Client Objectives

This section introduces the process of identifying desired and required returns, which should take place concurrently with the discussion of risk tolerances. In the end, the IPS must present a return objective that is attainable within the risk constraints of the portfolio.

Part IV - Constraints

All economic and operational constraints should be outlined in this section in order to properly tailor the portfolio without violating any client-imposed restrictions. These constraints include:

- Time Horizon
- Liquidity Requirements
- Taxes
- Legal and Regulatory Issues
- Unique Circumstances and Preferences

Part V - Asset Allocation

This section outlines the appropriate asset mix that meets the client's objectives and constraints as stated in this investment policy statement.

Part VI - Portfolio Monitoring and Reporting

This part sets forth the process and timing of investment monitoring as well as the schedule for performance review.

Part I - Purpose

The Investment Policy Statement (IPS) is designed to assist you and your Investment Advisor in effectively constructing, monitoring and evaluating the investments set forth within this IPS. Its purpose is to formally describe how your investment decisions are related to your goals and objectives while simultaneously adhering to any constraints. This exercise should produce realistic investment goals, and, equally important, a common vocabulary for discussion of risk and return.

Additionally, it should detail an investment structure for managing your portfolio. This structure will include various asset classes that are expected to produce an appropriate level of overall diversification and an appropriate risk-adjusted return over the investment time horizon.

Part II - Roles and Responsibilities

Investment Advisor: Jeffrey Harris

You have retained an objective, third party advisor to assist in the managing and implementation of your investment portfolio. Additionally, the Advisor will be responsible for guiding you through a disciplined investment process. The primary responsibilities of the Advisor are:

1. Prepare and maintain this Investment Policy Statement.

2. Provide risk/return profile.

3. Prudently recommend investment alternatives.

4. Avoid prohibited transactions and conflicts of interest.

5. Monitor and supervise the recommended investment vehicles.

6. Control and account for all investment expenses.

Investment Managers

Investment managers are responsible for making investment decisions based upon their predetermined process and philosophy. The specific duties and responsibilities of each manager are to:

1. Manage the assets in accordance with the guidelines and objectives set forth within the individual manager's marketing materials and/or RJCS Due Diligence research reports.

2. Vote promptly all proxies and related actions in a manner consistent with the long-term interest and objectives of the Client. Each investment manager shall keep detailed records of the voting of proxies and related actions and will comply with all applicable regulatory obligations.

3. Use the same care, skill, prudence and diligence under the prevailing circumstances that experienced investment professionals, acting in like capacity, and fully familiar with such matters, would use in like activities for like portfolios, with like aims, in accordance and compliance with the Prudent Investor Rule and all applicable laws, rules and regulations.

Custodians are responsible for the safekeeping of the Client's assets. The specific duties and responsibilities of the custodian are:

1. Provide monthly reports that detail transactions, cash flows, securities held and their current value, and change in value of each security and the overall portfolios since the previous report.

2. Maintain separate accounts by legal registration.

3. Value the holdings.

4. Collect all income and dividends owed to the Client.

5. Settle all transactions initiated by the Investment Managers.

Part III - Client Objectives

The process of identifying an appropriate return objective should take place concurrently with the discussion of risk tolerances. In the end, the IPS must present a return objective that is attainable within the risk constraints of the portfolio.

Return Objectives and Risk Tolerance:

Through consultation with your Investment Advisor, you have determined that a Balanced objective is most appropriate. The objective is to offer the potential for both capital appreciation and current income through a roughly 30% - 70% allocation to equities and a 30% - 70% allocation to fixed income investments.

When investing in capital markets, you must recognize and acknowledge that some risk must be assumed in order to achieve long-term investment objectives, and there are uncertainties and complexities associated with these markets. Through the investment objective selected, you are stating that you are comfortable with a moderate degree of risk.

The target average annual return on this portfolio is 6.0-8.5% net to the Whites after all fees and expenses are accounted for. Of course it is understood this cannot be guaranteed. Market forces, which cannot be controlled by the investment advisor or money managers, will dictate actual returns and may be higher or lower than the target return.

Part IV - Constraints

Time Horizon:

The minimum expected investment period should be at least five years for any portfolio containing equities. For any portfolio with less than a five-year time horizon, the portfolio should be comprised predominately of fixed income investments. Multi-stage time horizons have also been considered and properly addressed. You have stated that your time horizon is short (3-5 years). The primary stage is 1 to 5 years; the secondary stage is 1 to 5 years.

Liquidity Requirements:

With liquidity defined as either income needs, funding requirements, or as cash reserves to meet emergency needs, your liquidity requirement is low since you have other assets to draw from.

There will be a need for the investment earnings of this portfolio to meet some or all of your annual expenses. Expenses needed to be addressed in some form by this portfolio are determined to be $50,000 annually.

Anticipated future liquidity events are not a consideration at this point and should not be taken into consideration when constructing the allocation.

Taxes:

Tax structures that reduce the amount of total return that can be used for current needs or reinvested for future growth should be addressed. For taxable investors, tax considerations can influence the choice of investments as well as the timing of sales. Consideration should be given as to the appropriateness of both taxable and tax exempt investments. Your taxable implications are an issue, and should be taken into consideration when constructing the portfolio.

Comments:

The Whites would like to limit income tax liability as much as possible.

Legal and Regulatory Issues:

External factors imposed by governmental, regulatory or oversight authorities which constrain the investment decision-making process have been addressed. Prudent Investor Rules apply. The Prudent Investor Rules state that a fiduciary must:

1. Make investment and management decisions with respect to individual assets in the context of the investment portfolio as a whole and as part of an overall investment strategy, not in isolation.

2. Adhere to fundamental fiduciary duties of loyalty, impartiality, and prudence.

3. Maintain overall portfolio risk at a reasonable level. That is, risk and return objectives must be reasonable and suitable to the portfolio. The trade-off between risk and return is the fiduciary's central concern.

4. Provide for the reasonable diversification of investments.

5. Act with prudence in deciding whether and how to delegate authority to experts and in selecting supervising agents. Be cost-

conscious when investing. The fiduciary should incur only costs that are reasonable in amount and appropriate to the investment responsibilities of the fiduciary.

Unique Circumstances:

Unique circumstances may include guidelines for social or special purpose investing, assets legally restricted from sale, directed brokerage arrangements, and privacy concerns. Additionally, assets held outside the investment portfolio and not otherwise considered within this investment policy should be listed here.

Part V - Asset Allocation

The allocation that best satisfies your objectives and constraints, as stated in this investment policy statement, is a Balanced objective. You also realize that investing involves risk and there is no guarantee that this allocation will perform as expected.

	Lower Limit	Strategic Allocation	Upper Limit
(Non) Taxable Fixed Income	37%	47%	57%
Domestic Large-Cap Equity	20%	30%	40%
Small to Mid-Cap Equity	5%	10%	15%
International Equity	5%	10%	15%
Cash Equivalent	0%	3%	6%

Part VI - Portfolio Monitoring and Reporting

Investment performance must be periodically evaluated to assess progress towards the achievement of investment objectives. More importantly, as your objectives and constraints materially change, a review of this investment policy statement is recommended. Currently, an annual review is recommended.

INVESTMENT POLICY REVIEW

Your Advisor will review this IPS with you at least annually to determine whether stated investment objectives are still relevant. It is not expected that the IPS will change frequently. In particular, short-term changes in the financial markets should not require adjustments to the IPS. It is the obligation of the Client to notify all interested parties of any material changes that would alter the objectives or construction of this portfolio. If all interested parties are not notified of these material changes, then the current investment policy statement is invalid.

This IPS is not a contractual agreement of any kind and therefore by signing it you will not be bound to any arrangement. It is only meant to be a summary of the agreed-upon investment management techniques.

Prepared: _____

Approved: _____

_____   _____
ADVISOR   DATE

_____   _____
CLIENT   DATE

Appendix D

Sample Fee Schedule

Comprehensive Advisory Services Fee Schedule

Jeff Harris & Associates, Inc. believes that our clients are best served when our economic interests are aligned with theirs. Therefore we have chosen to serve our clients on a fee-for-service basis, instead of the traditional commission basis, which could create a conflict of interest.

Our professional fees are based on the amount of assets we manage for our clients, and volume discounts apply. Fees are annual, but charged quarterly, and may be tax deductible*. Since our compensation is directly tied to our clients' success, we have a strong vested interest to help clients preserve and protect assets while positioning them for prudent growth potential over time.

- Complete confidentiality
- Development of personalized investment portfolio (Investment Policy Statement)
- Implementation of personalized investment strategy
- Portfolio re-balancing as appropriate
- Monthly account statements
- Quarterly account review and summary
- Regular review of account holdings by independent advisor
- 24-hour access to account information via the Internet
- Annual account summary for tax reporting
- Consolidated account reporting showing all assets simultaneously
- Access to superior independent stock and mutual fund research
- Access to alternative investments
- Ongoing income tax reduction planning (with CPA)
- Estate analysis and document review (with attorney)
- Personal access to your own independent investment advisor
- Retirement planning
- Simplification of estate settlement for heirs
- Highly competitive annual fee schedule: 1.25% down to 0.10% of assets under management. Fee is annual, but billed quarterly.

* Management fees may be fully or partially tax deductible. See your tax professional for more information.

Glossary

After-Tax Return
The return on an investment after deducting taxes owed. The after-tax return on a taxable investment may be calculated as follows: pretax rate of return X (100% minus taxpayer's marginal income tax rate).

Asset Allocation
Dividing investment dollars among several different asset classes (e.g., cash, bonds, stocks, real estate) in order to pursue certain goals, such as balancing risk and return. Also known as "investment mix."

401(k) Plan
A defined contribution plan in which an employee may elect, as an alternative to receiving taxable cash in the form of compensation or a bonus, to contribute pre-tax dollars to a qualified tax-deferred retirement plan. Also known as a cash or deferred arrangement (CODA) or salary reduction plan.

Balanced Fund
A mutual fund that invests in a mix of common stock, preferred stock, and bonds in an effort to achieve both growth and preservation of capital within the same fund.

Basis Point
The general method used for quoting bond yields and interest rates. A single basis point is one-hundredth (1/100) of 1 percent (0.01%). Therefore, an interest rate of 5 percent (5%) equals 500 basis points.

Bear Market
A market in which prices are generally decreasing. It got that name from the fact that when bears fight, they first stand up, then drop down to attack their enemy.

Benchmarking
An investment strategy that allows you to measure the performance of your portfolio by comparison to a standardized index, such as the S&P 500 or the NASDAQ Composite. The more closely the index mirrors your own portfolio, the more effective this strategy is.

Beneficiary
An individual designated in a will to receive an inheritance, or the individual designated to receive the proceeds of an insurance policy, retirement account, trust, or other asset upon the death of another individual.

Bequest
A gift of personal property by will. A testamentary disposition of real property is typically referred to as a "devise." A bequest may be absolute (without condition), conditional (effective only upon the occurrence or nonoccurrence of a certain event), general (payable out of the general assets of the testator), or specific (specially designated property). Also known as a legacy.

Blend Fund
A mutual fund that spreads its holdings over more than one asset class. A typical blend fund might invest in a combination of stocks, bonds, and money market securities. These funds typically provide greater diversification than funds that limit their holdings to one asset class.

Blue Chip Stock
Common stock of a nationally known company that has a long record of profit growth and dividend payments, and a reputation for quality management, products, and services. Examples of blue chip stocks include IBM, General Electric, and DuPont. Blue chip stocks typically are relatively high-priced and low-yielding.

Bond
A debt instrument sold by companies, governments, and institutions in order to raise money. A bond is like an IOU from the borrower to the lender. The investor who buys a bond is lending a certain amount of money (the bond's face value) to the bond issuer. The bond issuer is agreeing to repay the principal amount of the loan at a certain time (maturity date). Prior to maturity, most bonds also periodically pay interest to the investor.

Bond Fund
A mutual fund that invests in corporate, municipal, or Treasury bonds. Most bond funds provide a steady stream of current income through regular dividends. These dividends are based on interest payments made by the individual bonds in the fund's portfolio.

Bond Rating
A measure of the quality and safety of a bond. There are rating service firms that specialize in rating bonds, usually on a letter-grade scale, based on the financial stability of the bond issuer. Typically, the higher the rating, the less likely the issuer is to default on interest and principal payments.

Bull Market
A rising market, or a market in which prices are generally increasing for stocks, bonds, or commodities. It got that name from the fact that when bulls fight, they drop down low then drive upward with their horns to attack their enemy.

Capital Gains

For investment purposes, the increase in the value of an asset over time. For income tax purposes, the profit realized on the sale of a capital asset as defined by the Internal Revenue Code. Short-term capital gains (assets held for 12 months or less) are taxed at ordinary income rates. Long-term capital gains (assets held longer than 12 months) are taxed at capital gains tax rates.

Capital Gains Tax

Tax on the gain realized from the sale of capital assets such as a home, investments, and business interests. Assets held longer than 12 months generate long-term capital gains, which are generally subject to favorable tax rates. Assets held 12 months or less generate short-term capital gains, which are subject to regular income tax rates. Capital gains tax rates also apply to certain dividends received by individual shareholders from domestic and qualified foreign corporations (for taxable years beginning after 2002 and before 2009).

Cash Equivalent

An asset that can be converted to currency on short notice. For financial purposes, instruments and investments of such high liquidity that they are virtually cash, such as money market funds and Treasury bills.

Cash Reserve

An emergency or contingency fund (or credit) set aside and held in an easily accessible form (such as a savings account) for the purpose of meeting emergency expenses and/or short-term cash flow needs.

Charitable Gift

A contribution of cash or property to (or for the use of) a qualified charitable organization. A federal income tax deduction is allowed for the tax year in which the gift is made.

Charitable Remainder Trust

A trust that provides for a specified distribution to one or more beneficiaries, at least one of which is not a charity. The distribution must be paid at least annually for life or for a term of years, with a remainder interest to be held for the benefit of (or paid over to) one or more qualified charities. The specified distribution must be either (1) a sum certain that is not less than 5 percent and not more than 50 percent of the initial net fair market value of all property placed in trust, or (2) a fixed percentage that is not less than 5 percent and not more than 50 percent of the net fair market value of the trust assets, valued annually.

Closed-End Fund
A mutual fund that issues a limited number of shares for sale to the investing public. Shares usually cannot be redeemed, but are traded on the stock exchanges or over-the-counter markets. Supply and demand determine the price of a closed-end fund.

Commission
The fee paid to a broker, financial planner, insurance agent, or other licensed professional for executing a trade or other transaction. The fee is typically a percentage of the dollar value of the transaction.

Common Stock
Units of ownership of a corporation. Common stockholders are typically entitled to vote on the selection of directors and other matters. However, common stock is generally secondary to preferred stock in the payment of dividends and the liquidation of company assets.

Corporate Bond
A bond issued by a corporation, rather than by a government. Unlike government bonds, which may be tax exempt, corporate bonds are fully taxable by federal, state, and local governments. However, they normally pay more interest.

Corporation
A legal business entity that is separate and distinct from its owners. Ownership is represented by transferable shares of stock. A corporation is allowed to own property, incur liabilities, sell securities, sue or be sued, and file its own separate tax return.

Current Yield
A measurement of a bond's rate of return. The bond's annual interest income compared to the bond's current market price, expressed as a percentage. In mathematical terms, it is the coupon rate divided by the market price. Also known as yield.

Death Benefit
The amount payable, as stated in a life insurance policy, to the designated beneficiary(ies) upon the death of the insured. The amount paid is the face value, plus any riders, less any outstanding loans and interest due.

Defined Benefit Pension Plan
A qualified employer-sponsored retirement plan that guarantees a specified benefit level at retirement.

Defined Contribution Plan
A qualified employer-sponsored retirement plan in which each participant has an individual account and the amount the employer contributes to each account is defined, usually as a percentage of compensation, in the plan document.

Diversification
Balancing an investment portfolio by purchasing securities of different industries or classes in order to spread risk; the underlying premise being that it is unlikely that all investments in a portfolio will move in the same direction at the same time. Thus, the loss from one investment will be offset by the gain from a different investment.

Dividend
Distribution of a company's earnings to shareholders, generally on a quarterly basis, paid in cash or additional shares of the company's stock. The dividend amount per share is decided by the company's board of directors. Dividends must be declared as income by the shareholder in the year received.

Donor
The person who executes a deed to convey title to property or who creates a trust. Also called a creator, settlor, grantor, or trustor.

Dow Jones Industrial Average
A price-weighted average of 30 actively-traded blue chip stocks, primarily industrials but including American Express and Verizon. It is the oldest and most widely quoted of all the stock market indicators. The average is quoted in points, not dollars.

Employee Retirement Income Security Act (ERISA)
A federal law, passed in 1974, that governs the operation of private pension and benefit plans. A major component of the law is its emphasis on fiduciary duty for employers.

Equity-Income Fund
A stock mutual fund that invests solely or primarily in dividend-paying stocks. These funds are typically suitable for investors who seek current income.

Estate
Generally, the assets and liabilities of a person, particularly a deceased person. For estate tax purposes, interests in real or personal property that a person owns or controls at death (the gross taxable estate). Property passing under a will is known as the probate estate.

Expense Ratio
The amount that mutual fund shareholders pay annually for the fund's fees and expenses, expressed as a percentage of the total shareholder assets. This ratio typically ranges from .5 percent to 3 percent or more of shareholder assets, and can be found in the fund's prospectus.

Federal Estate Tax
A federal tax imposed on the value of an individual's property at death. The amount of property each person can exclude from estate tax is:
* 2005: $1.5 million
* 2006: $2 million
* 2007: $2 million
* 2008: $2 million
* 2009: $3.5 million
* 2010: estate tax is repealed
* 2011 and thereafter: $1 million (estate tax is reinstated)

Fees and Expenses
Costs other than sales charges you incur when you invest in a mutual fund (e.g., management and trustee's fees). Total fees and expenses depend on the fund, ranging anywhere from .5 percent to 3 percent or more of your investment.

Fiduciary
One who has the legal duty to act primarily for the benefit of others; one who acts in a capacity of trust. A person or institution who manages property for others and is obligated to exercise a certain standard of care regarding such management. Executors of estates, trustees of trusts, and receivers in bankruptcy are examples of fiduciaries.

Fund Family
A group of mutual funds offered by an investment company. A typical fund family includes several types of stock, bond, and money market funds that pursue various investment objectives (e.g., capital growth, dividend income, or a combination of growth and income). Many fund companies allow investors to move money around within their family of funds free of charge.

Gift
A voluntary transfer of property to another in exchange for nothing or property of less value. Usually refers to transfers made during life.

Global Fund
A mutual fund that invests in securities (e.g., stocks or bonds) from both the United States and other nations around the world. This is in contrast to an international fund, which invests exclusively in foreign-based securities.

Government Bond
A bond issued by the U.S. Treasury or another federal agency and backed by the full faith and credit of the U.S. government. These bonds typically make interest payments at regular intervals and pay a specified amount (the face amount) to the bondholder at maturity.

Growth Fund
A stock mutual fund whose main goal is to provide its shareholders with long-term capital appreciation. Growth funds invest in stocks that typically rise and fall faster than the market as a whole and pay few, if any, dividends.

Growth and Income Fund
A mutual fund that invests in stocks with a history of consistent growth and steady dividend payments. These funds typically experience moderate price volatility.

Hedge Fund
A mutual fund that seeks to enhance return by using sophisticated "hedging" techniques, such as leverage and selling short, that aren't used by other types of funds. Since the minimum investment is typically very high, few individual investors have the resources needed to invest in a hedge fund. Most hedge fund investors are institutions or very wealthy individuals.

Income Tax
Annual tax on the net income of an individual or corporation that is levied by the federal government, most states, and some local governments.

Index
A statistical composite that measures changes in the economy or in financial markets by measuring the ups and downs of stock, bond, and commodities markets, and reflecting market prices and the number of shares outstanding for the companies in the index. Some well-known indexes include the New York Stock Exchange Composite Index, S&P 500 and the American Stock Exchange Composite Index.

Index Fund
A mutual fund that attempts to match the performance of a broad-based portfolio (e.g., the S&P 500, NASDAQ Composite, or a bond index) by investing in the same securities. Because index funds require little active management, they tend to have lower fees and expenses than other funds.

Indexing

An investment strategy that attempts to match the performance of a broad-based index of securities, such as the S&P 500. To achieve this goal, the investor designs a portfolio that mirrors (as closely as possible) the index being tracked.

International Bond

A bond issued by a company based outside the United States. Foreign currency fluctuations and overseas interest rates are among the factors that influence international bond prices.

International Stock

Stock issued by a company based outside the United States. These stocks can be volatile, depending on foreign economic conditions and currency fluctuations. International stocks may help offset investment losses when the U.S. stock market takes a downturn.

IRA (Individual Retirement Arrangement)

Personal, tax-deferred retirement account that an individual can set up and fund with earned income up to a maximum of $4,000 per year for tax years 2005-2007 ($4,500 in 2005, $5,000 in 2006-2007 if age 50 or older due to a "catch-up" provision in the law). Under certain conditions, the contributions are tax deductible. Interest accumulation is not taxed until funds are withdrawn from the IRA.

Irrevocable Trust

A trust that cannot be revoked or amended. Once the trust agreement is executed, its provisions are fixed. No property can be removed and no terms can be changed.

Junk Bond

A bond rated BB or lower by Standard & Poor's or Ba or lower by Moody's, two nationally recognized securities rating organizations. Junk bonds are generally more volatile and less liquid than higher-rated bonds, and thus involve a greater degree of risk. These bonds appeal to investors who are looking for higher yields than less-volatile investments offer, and who are willing to accept the risks. Also known as a high-yield bond.

Large Cap

Short for a large-capitalization stock or stock fund that invests in the stock of well-established companies. A well-established company is considered to be a company with market capitalization (dollar value of outstanding shares) of at least $5 billion (Morningstar figure).

Living Trust
A revocable or irrevocable trust created during the life of the grantor. Also known as an inter vivos trust.

Load
The sales charge assessed to the account owner of a mutual fund or other investment. The load is usually a percentage of the transaction amount, and can be either front-end (paid at the time of purchase) or back-end (paid at the time of withdrawal).

Market Risk
Losses due to the falling prices of securities; type of systematic risk referring to the possibility that an investment will lose value over time because of a general decline in financial markets, or in a specific sector of the market, which is brought on by outside forces. Such forces include war, disaster, presidential elections, and changes in the interest rate and employment rate. A good example of market risk was experienced on "Black Monday," October 19, 1987, the day stock market prices fell by almost one-fourth.

Market Timing
Moving assets among certain types of stocks, bonds, or other securities to take advantage of anticipated trends in the financial markets. Market timers attempt to predict the future movement of those markets based on recent price information, the general direction of interest rates and the economy, and other data.

Mid Cap
Short for a "middle capitalization" stock or stock fund that invests in the stock of medium-sized companies. A medium-sized company is considered to be a company with market capitalization (dollar value of outstanding shares) between $1 billion and $5 billion (Morningstar figure).

Modern Portfolio Theory
An investment theory that emphasizes a diversified portfolio as the key to successful investing. According to this theory, the investor's goal should be to purchase investments that provide the highest possible return at the lowest possible risk.

Money Market Fund
An open-end mutual fund that invests exclusively in money market securities. These funds have a fixed price per share of $1, but the interest rate may vary based on market conditions. Money market funds sold by banks are FDIC-insured.

Municipal Bond
A bond issued by a state or local government, usually to raise money for new roads, schools, or other public projects. The interest paid on municipal bonds is usually exempt from federal, state, and local taxes.

Mutual Fund
Corporation or trust, managed by an investment advisor, that pools money from shareholders and invests it in securities, such as stocks, bonds, options, commodities, and/or money market securities. Registered with the Securities and Exchange Commission under the Investment Company Act, mutual funds offer investors the advantages of diversification and professional management, for which they charge a management fee.

NASDAQ Composite Index
A broad-based composite of the market values of all foreign and domestic companies listed on the National Association of Securities Dealers Automated Quotation (NASDAQ) system. Thousands of companies are traded on this technology-heavy index.

No-Load Fund
A mutual fund purchased by an investor directly from an investment company. Because a broker isn't used, these funds carry no sales charges or redemption fees. However, some no-load funds charge a 12b-1 distribution fee. No-load funds are listed in the financial pages with the abbreviation "NL."

Open-End Fund
A mutual fund that continually creates new shares to accommodate investor demand. Shares may be redeemed at any time for their current market value. The vast majority of mutual funds are open-end funds.

P/E Ratio
Price/earnings ratio. The ratio of a company's stock price per share to its profits in a given year. (The P/E equation is market capitalization [market value of outstanding common stock], divided by net earnings [gross revenue, minus expenses and taxes].) It is the most common measure used to analyze stock. Companies with a P/E ratio over 20 are typically young, fast-growing firms with relatively low earnings.

Portfolio
An assortment of investment assets held by an investor, such as cash, stocks, bonds, and real estate. Ideally designed to achieve diversification, balancing risk and return.

Preferred Stock

A class of company stock that has preferential rights over common stock in the payment of dividends and the liquidation of assets, but typically without voting rights (although it may be converted to common stock with voting rights).

Pre-tax Return

The return on an investment before taxes have been paid. The pre-tax return is always higher than the after-tax return, unless the investment is tax-free (e.g., a municipal bond).

Profit-Sharing Plan

A type of defined contribution plan in which an employer contributes an amount of money that can be related to a company's annual profits. The amount can be discretionary or determined by a preset formula.

Prospectus

A legal document offering securities or mutual fund shares for sale. It must explain the offer, including the terms, planned use of monies, as well as other information needed to make an informed decision, such as sales charges and management fees. Traditionally, prospectuses have been nearly impossible to read because of legal and investment jargon. In recent years, the SEC has promulgated rules designed to make prospectuses more readable and easier for the average investor to understand.

Qualified Plan

A deferred compensation plan set up by an employer for employees that receives certain tax benefits, as provided by the Employee Retirement Income Security Act (ERISA). Some plans, such as a profit-sharing or pension plan, provide for employer contributions and may also allow employee contributions. Other plans, such as a matching 401(k) plan, provide for both employee and employer contributions. These plans are called "qualified" because they must comply with a number of complex rules to "qualify" for preferential tax treatment.

Real Estate Investment Trust (REIT)

A business entity that invests in real estate, or in mortgages on real estate. Similar to a mutual fund, the money of numerous investors is pooled to make selected long-term real estate investments. Any investment income generated by the REIT is passed through to the individual investors.

Rebalance

To restore an investment portfolio to its original asset allocation. For example, a portfolio has 50 percent of its value in stocks and 50 percent in bonds. Due to a rise in stocks over the next year, stocks now make up 60 percent of the portfolio's value and bonds only 40 percent. To rebalance the portfolio, the investor can buy more bonds and/or sell some of the stocks in the portfolio.

Risk

The possibility that an investment will return less than expected or lose principal. In insurance, the possibility of a loss of life or property.

Risk-Averse

Describes an investor who wants to avoid risk altogether, or one who is willing to assume risk only if adequately rewarded for it. To some degree, all investors are risk-averse. Given a number of investment choices, each providing the same return, a prudent investor will choose the lowest-risk investment choices.

Risk Management

Procedures to minimize the adverse effect of a possible financial loss by identifying potential sources of loss, measuring the financial consequences of a loss occurring, and using controls to minimize actual losses or their financial consequences

Risk Tolerance

The degree to which an investor can endure price volatility and fluctuation in the market. Investors with a high risk tolerance can handle large and frequent swings in the value of their portfolios. Those with a low risk tolerance become anxious during periods of volatility and are often described as risk-averse.

Russell 2000 Index

A stock index, compiled and published by the Frank Russell Company, that tracks the daily value of small-company stocks in various industries. It includes the 2,000 smallest companies in the Russell 3000 Index.

S&P 500 Index

A broad-based stock market index created by Standard & Poor's Corporation (S&P) to track daily value changes in the stock market or a segment of the market. This index includes 500 blue chip stocks considered to be a benchmark of the overall stock market.

Securities and Exchange Commission (SEC)

A federal agency created by the Securities Exchange Act of 1934 that oversees and regulates the securities industry. The SEC's regulations are aimed at promoting full public disclosure and protecting the public from malpractice in the industry.

Small Cap

Short for a small-capitalization stock or stock fund that invests in the stock of smaller companies that generally have low revenues but high growth potential. A small company can be considered to be a company with market capitalization (dollar value of outstanding shares) under $1 billion (Morningstar figure).

Tax Basis

The original cost of an asset, adjusted for additions and/or accumulated depreciation. Used to calculate gain or loss for tax purposes.

Tax Bracket

The category into which you fall for federal income tax purposes based on the tax rate that would apply to your next dollar of income. Under a progressive tax system, increases in taxable income generally put the taxpayer in a higher tax bracket with higher income tax rates. Currently, there are six tax brackets for individuals: 10 percent, 15 percent, 25 percent, 28 percent, 33 percent, and 35 percent.

Time Horizon

The length of time one expects to remain in a particular investment or investment vehicle. For example, an investor who expects to retire in four years may have a short time horizon with respect to his or her 401(k) plan. A young investor in the 401(k) plan may have a much longer time horizon.

Treasury Note

A security guaranteed by the U.S. government that has a maturity of one to ten years. Denominations range from $1,000 to $1 million or more, depending on the duration of the note purchased. They pay interest semiannually that is exempt from state and local (but not federal) taxes and repay principal at maturity.

Trust

A legal entity in which a trustee, holds title to and manages property for the benefit of a beneficiary. A trust created during the trustor's lifetime is called a living or inter vivos trust, and a trust created by a will is called a testamentary trust.

Value Fund
A mutual fund that invests in value stocks. These are stocks that seem undervalued because their market price is low in relation to the company's earnings, cash flow, overall financial condition, and other factors.

Volatility
The tendency of an investment's price to increase or decrease over time. High volatility refers to large, rapid, or unexpected price fluctuations, while low volatility refers to smaller or more gradual price changes. Volatility is a key measurement of risk. Generally, the higher the volatility of an investment, the higher the risk associated with that investment.

Yield
The yearly rate of return on an investment, expressed as a percentage. A bond's yield is the annual interest rate divided by the market price; as the price drops, the yield rises, and vice versa. For stocks, the yield is the annual dividends divided by the purchase price.

Glossary information courtesy of Forefield. www.forefield.com/company

This book would not have been possible without the help of the following people and organizations:

Mike Hernacki, Editor
michaelhernacki@cox.net

Mark Beaudry, Cover Design
http://www.markbeaudry.com/

COVI Communications, Production
coviusa@cox.net

Printed by:
Color House Graphics, Grand Rapids, Michigan
http://www.colorhousegraphics.com

Book Consultant:
Dan Poynter
http://www.parapublishing.com

Publicist:
Paul Krupin
http://www.imediafax.com